Shaggy Dog *Tales*

Shaggy Dog *Tales*

58 1/2 Years of Reportage

Paul Ress

Library of Congress Control Number:		2006907018
ISBN 10:	Hardcover	1-4257-2747-6
	Softcover	1-4257-2746-8
ISBN 13:	Hardcover	978-1-4257-2747-5
	Softcover	978-1-4257-2746-8

To order additional copies of this book, contact:
Xlibris Corporation
1-888-795-4274
www.Xlibris.com
Orders@Xlibris.com
34128

Contents

For
Sue Pfiffner
without whose perspicacious editing and enormous practical assistance
this book would never have seen the light of day

Foreword

When Paul came to Europe, in the spring of 1947, a recently demobbed US soldier and a flunked student from Columbia Law School, he was clear about one thing: he wanted to write. Not novels, not plays, not poetry, but journalism, the old-fashioned reporting that had made its name with H.L. Mencken, Dorothy Thompson and Vincent Sheean. And write this kind of journalism he did, clearly, honestly, and with no attempt to score points or to produce stories designed to exalt the writer.

Though his politics were always firmly to the left, and he had trouble believing that any decent person could feel any sympathy with the right, it mattered to him to be fair. He was also self-evidently courteous and kindly and had a passion for shaggy dogs. But Paul brought to his stories something else very much his own: a gently mocking, generous-spirited sense of humor.

He has become legendary—to the despair of some—for his puns. "Eggs-en-Provence" and "modus vivaldi" are but two of the hundreds—thousands?—of terrible puns that have entertained (and maddened) his friends and captivated (and appalled) his editors.

Not surprising, then, that with this delight in punning came a lifelong obsession with words, their use and misuse, their absurdities and derivations. Paul, avid collector of all forms of humor, intentional or otherwise, to be found in modern journalism, has always had a keen and deflating eye for the obvious, the pretentious and the ridiculous.

This has led him, over the years, to search for painted beehives in Slovenia and to scour the Corsican hillsides for prehistoric statues, though his preference has always been for the lunchtime interview, conducted over excellent food and wine in a restaurant. Perhaps uniquely for a man who has lived for many years on his own, Paul has never been known to cook a meal. In one of his apartments in Geneva, the kitchen was turned into a spare room.

It is no accident that Paul has wound up in Geneva, one of the most dog-friendly cities in the world, where large sheepdogs dine out in restaurants and travel as full-paying citizens on buses. Paul's fondness for animals extends to cats, but not much further. When he decided to follow in Stevenson's footsteps in the Cévennes, he fell out so profoundly with his rented donkey that he abandoned his journey after three exhausting, quarrelsome days.

Unlike many reporters, Paul always said that he would never write an autobiography. This collection of charming and funny pieces, many about a lost and vanishing world, must stand for one, and they convey wonderfully well the essentially modest and humorous nature of a man for whom friendship and good conversation has always been more interesting than fame.

Caroline Moorehead

Caroline Moorehead is a biographer, a journalist, a book reviewer and a defender of human rights. Among her dozen books are "Dunant's Dream," a definitive history of the International Committee of the Red Cross, biographies of Bertrand Russell, Heinrich Schliemann, Freya Stark and Martha Gellhorn, and most recently, a moving study of refugees, "Human Cargo."

Freedom of the P.RESS

One evening in the south of France Graham Greene said to me, "I suppose that like most American journalists you plan to write the great American novel." I replied that I labored under no such illusion. "Very fortunate," he added, "because it has already been written." "Which is to say?" I inquired. Greene replied, "Huckleberry Finn."

Not once since that conversation has it occurred to me to try to write any kind of book, much less the "great American novel." During a span of almost 30 years as a journalist for major media, I was convinced that there was no life after journalism. Even losing my job as a reporter three times did not change my mind.

What did alter my outlook was the discovery of international and non-governmental environmental and public health organizations in and around the United Nations in Geneva that were doing good things.

Writing about their activities and seeing them reported not in one newspaper or magazine but in hundreds of publications and on radio and television stations around the world, was a satisfying experience. It was journalistic writing, and, sometimes, the press releases and feature stories really did make things move. Two examples.

A simple World Health Organization press release on arsenic in the drinking water in Bangladesh led to an investigation on the spot by a reporter of a major American newspaper. His syndicated story caught the attention of a Nordic government which agreed to finance efforts to try to rid the wells of the arsenic.

Another story—for UNICEF this time—concerned premature or underweight babies in Colombia in a region where hospitals had no incubators. The mother carried her baby close to her body beneath her sweater or dress rather like a kangaroo with a baby in her pouch. It saved their lives. They came to be known as "kangaroo babies." A respected, large-circulation British newspaper read the feature, sent a team with a doctor, a nurse, a reporter, and a photographer to Colombia, and published a big cover story on the technique in their Sunday magazine. Articles about "kangaroo babies" keep popping up here and there, and the kangaroo system has spread.

The stories and the anecdotes in this book illustrate these two kinds of journalism over a period of more than half a century. Changing times lead to changes in tone and approach in writing, but a good story is always a good story.

Those First Post-War Years

One day in 1948 the Paris Herald's Palais de Justice stringer phoned Eric Hawkins, the managing editor. "Pierrot le Fou [Crazy Pete] has just escaped from the police and is running around the roof of the law courts," he cried. "Get someone down here quick!" Eric called in Bob Haney who was not only the city editor but the entire city staff. "The worst criminal in France is running loose at the Palais de Justice," he explained. "Get there fast. Take the métro!"

With my salary of $26 a month (eh oui, per month) I would have taken the métro, too.

After joyfully flunking out of Columbia Law School, I had found a job on the Paris Herald in April 1947, tearing wire service copy from teletype machines and feeding it to editors. Maybe that was worth only $26 a month, but no one could have lived on it. My army savings of $700 went first and then I cashed in my $160 return-trip ticket on the Queen Mary.

When and how could I ever afford to go back to the United States, I wondered. Fortunately, the editor, Geoff Parsons, had been a founder of the Newspaper Guild in Boston, and although now management, he remembered his days as "a working newspaperman." Even though the newspaper wasn't rich, Geoff gave everyone a free trip home.

Those early post-war years, when one looks back at them, had a surprisingly prim and proper tone. Jean-Paul Sartre's play, "La Putain Respectueuse" (The respectful whore), was on everybody's lips but all over Paris the billboards advertised "La P . . . Respectueuse." By ricochet this ban on calling a putain a putain got me into trouble with Eric Hawkins.

I had graduated to reviewing plays and to an almost livable wage. Along came John Ford's Elizabethan drama, "'Tis Pity She's a Whore," which the French prudently and inaccurately translated as "Dommage qu'elle soit une prostituée." In my review, I put the correct title in parentheses next to the French title. Eric spotted it on the galley proofs in the composing room in the basement. He ran up to the editorial room and angrily asked who had done the theater review.

"The correct translation of 'prostituée' is prostitute and not whore," he roared. "But, Eric," I tried to object, "you can't change the name of . . . ." "Don't but me, young fellow, I know more about French now than you will ever know." We should have compromised with "'Tis Pity She's a W . . .".

During my years on the Paris Herald (1947-1950) we all worked a six-day week, with only Saturday off. The staff petitioned management to make it a five-day week. "Absolutely impossible," retorted Eric, "you can't put out a paper six days a week with a staff that works five." O tempora, o mores.

The Paris Herald's most illustrious alumnus arrived in 1948. One of the first assignments Eric Hawkins gave Art Buchwald was to go to Deauville on a summer weekend and to describe the social scene in the fashionable English Channel resort.

Art's column—the first of about 8,000 penned in Paris and Washington— spoke of the necessity of staying at the Golf or the Normandie Hotel because there, said he, you would be hobnobbing with such pillars of society as the Maharani of Baroda, the Aga Khan and the Begum, Gianni Agnelli, the Duke and Duchess of Windsor, Henry Ford III, and E. Philips Ashworth, the ex-city solicitor of Philadelphia.

From the hotel you had to go to a certain restaurant because there, and nowhere else, would you encounter the Maharani of Baroda, the Aga Khan and the Begum, Gianni Agnelli, and tutti quanti, including, of course, E. Philips Ashworth, the ex-city solicitor of Philadelphia.

Art then took his readers to the famous casino of Deauville where one met . . . and there followed the now-familiar list. One couldn't retire after gambling at the casino, it was essential to have a nightcap at Beau Brummel's. There, need I add, one met the identical cast of characters.

When Buchwald turned in his copy to the managing editor, Eric read it carefully and said to him, "It's good, but why do you keep repeating all those names?"

A case of Art imitating life? In any event, Art put E. Philips Ashworth, the ex-city solicitor of Philadelphia, on the map if not in the social register, and Ashworth was immensely grateful to him.

In spite of his immediate popularity, Art remained a modest columnist. He liked to toss his column on the copy desk and say to the chief copy reader or "slot man," Roy McMullen, "Mac, fix it up any way you see fit." Most journalists were more in love with their own prose than Art ever was.

McMullen had a team of bright headline writers, one of whom, Fred Shaw, specialized in rhyming heads. Given a story about a woman of 90 in Illinois who had seen her first play, Shaw wrote the headline:

"Woman in Decatur
Goes to Theater"

Unquestionably the most "Frenchified" of Paris Herald Americans, Bob Haney spoke absolutely accentless, elegant French. The only criticism I ever heard of it was from a native French speaker that "it sounds like Académie Française French, it's too good." Bob himself maintained that he "spoke better, purer French in Ames, Iowa, than after I had been living in Paris for six months. My French was contaminated by the French." Bob was (by far) the best man at my marriage, and no one at the Passy city hall suspected he wasn't French.

A lover of the Midi (the South of France) and what he called the "pastis-filtered sunlight of Arles," Bob was one of the few staffers to own a car, a black Citroën "traction-avant."

One day he received a disagreeable assignment: do a piece on American cars displayed at the Paris Automobile Salon for the paper's advertising supplement on the show. But what about the wall between advertising copy and news on an American newspaper, he grumbled? He went but he wrote the story his own way.

At a time when there were very, very few French cars in the streets of Paris, and virtually no American ones, he wrote in the last, unnoticed paragraph of his story: "There are now so many American cars whirling around the Place de la Concorde and around the Arc de Triomphe that the names of Cadillac, La Salle and Chevrolet have passed into the French language."

From the Paris Herald, I migrated to the Chicago Tribune. My boss there, Hank Wales, often warned me: "If I ask you to do a story, don't just read or talk to people on the phone about it—go do it! Then you can decently write about it. And that goes for any reportage." So when he sent me to do a story about coal mining in northern France, I joined the miners deep in the pits.

Sidewalk Tennis in Paris and the Riviera

When I first arrived in Paris, I discovered a new sport: tennis-barbe (tennis-beard). It was played by two friends seated at a sidewalk café. When you spotted someone with a beard passing by, you exclaimed "15" or "30-love" or "deuce" or wherever you were at in the game. As beards were rather rare in those days, a set could go on for quite a long time. Today, in these bearded times, a set might not last the time to sip one apéritif.

One day I told a friend, Colette Gallois, about this Parisian sport. Colette, who came from an upper-class family in Cannes, but didn't share their snobbish values, said, "Oh, we play a similar game on the Riviera, but we call it tennis-bretelle [tennis-strap]."

Around 1936, workers on the first paid vacations in their lives—thanks to the leftwing Popular Front government—arrived by the thousands for a summer holiday on the Riviera.

"The upper class resented these badly-dressed workers in their strapped underwear invading *their* Côte d'Azur," Colette explained. "That's when they invented the snobbish game of tennis-bretelle. When you were sitting at a sidewalk café, every time you saw a worker in a characteristic undershirt, you shouted '15' or 'deuce' or 'match point.'" I prefer the Parisian version of sidewalk tennis.

*　　*　　*

"Punning is an art of harmonious jingling upon words"
Jonathan Swift (1667-1745)

Southern Iranian food—Khomeni grits

In Dublin an active retiree is called a recycled teenager

Anyone suggesting Andorra should have its own stamps would be a Johnny-come-philately

Drinks with a German woman friend—a gin and teutonic

In conversation with Jacques Cousteau about the state of the Mediterranean: Let's let dugongs be dugongs

Corsican Menhirs—Don't Take
Them for Granite

"Slowly, painfully, cutting through the thick Corsican underbrush with machetes, we crawled up the hill. Suddenly, I found myself shoulder to shoulder with a prehistoric statue. It was lying face down. You can imagine the suspense and my emotion, as we cautiously turned it right side up. The granite face was clearly sculptured. It wasn't stylized, but that of an individual."

So said Roger Grosjean, the French archeologist, who had discovered the first of 17 menhir statues on a hillock in the hamlet of Filitosa, near Propriano, 30 miles south of Napoleon's birthplace in Ajaccio. All faced downward and were made of granite. That was 52 years ago in 1954.

Today, around 100 menhir statues have been found, dug up and put in a standing position in Corsica. On average they measure 2.62 meters high (close to nine feet). Considering that almost two feet lie underground, the visible part of the menhir resembles in height a very tall human being, for example, a basketball player. Some menhirs, like the one at Santa Maria, stand 3.75 meters or over 12 feet. Others reach four meters or 13 feet. Most menhirs weigh a ton, but a few can weigh as much as 2½ tons.

The name "menhir" derives from the Breton words "men" for stone, and "hir" for long. The term "menhir" has caught on, although modern archeologists, like Franck Leandri, much prefer "pierre dressée," which translates to upright stone or perhaps standing stone. A bit of confusion can arise over the term "pierres dressées" because Corsicans sometimes call them "stantari," i.e., petrified persons, for tradition has them petrified for having transgressed the moral code of society.

With carbon-14 tests, weapons and other datable archeological finds, Grosjean dated Filitosa's menhir-statues between 1400 BC and 1200 BC. In other words they preceded the golden age of Greek sculpture and of Etruscan art by 700 to 900 years. They are at least 3,200 to 3,400 years old!

When archeologists and art historians were first confronted with the sculptured Filitosa menhirs, and told by Grosjean of their 14th to 12th century BC origins, they usually exclaimed, "Surely you mean the fifth, and not the 14th or 12th centuries BC?" Today no one argues with Grosjean's menhir dating, unless it is to say that the earliest known upright stones in Corsica date from the end of the fifth millennium before the Christian era, i.e., around 4100 BC. Recent research by Andre D'Anna and Henri Marchesi established this.

"The Corsican menhirs are the oldest, individualized, sculptured, monumental statues in Europe," Grosjean maintained. "They are as important for sculpture as the cave drawings of Lascaux in southwestern France and Altamira in northern Spain are for the origins of painting.

"Admittedly, there was earlier neolithic sculpture but it was totemic in nature. Corsican menhirs are realistic and naturalistic, not stylized like Egyptian statues and they're not divinities. When you look at the face of a Corsican menhir, you know that it represents somebody, an individual to whom you wish you could give a name."

It is no exaggeration to say that one Filitosa menhir looks like the French poet, Baudelaire, while another resembles the Swiss-born French actor, Michel Simon. Most astonishing, one of the Filitosa menhirs bears a striking resemblance to George Washington.

In Franck Leandri's opinion the individualistic menhirs are intended to resemble chiefs, illustrious warriors, heroes probably, whom their peoples wished to honor with granite monuments.

The indigenous Corsican sculptors went to a great deal of time and trouble fashioning the facial features of menhirs in relief instead of merely engraving them. To sculpt a nose or a chin, for instance, they were obliged to chisel and rub off a lot of hard rock. Since they didn't have iron tools, they worked with round, white quartz. "It must have taken them many months to turn that granite into a statue," said Grosjean.

Just how arduous a task Corsicans cut out for themselves is suggested by an experiment Grosjean organized. To join the head and chest of a menhir, he hired a Sardinian specialist equipped with Swedish steel tools to dig a hole in each chunk of granite. Each hole measured four inches in diameter and six inches in depth. It took the Sardinian stone craftsman eight days to do the minor job with remarkable tools.

In the beginning, the menhir statues simply separated the head from the body with a neck. Later, shoulders were traced in the granite. Then facial traits appeared. Finally, artists sculpted details in the body down to arms and hands and ears. The facial features in particular, but the swords and daggers as well, are much clearer and more expressive on sunny days, of which Corsica has more than a fair share, than under a gray sky. "Literally, from one minute to another," said Grosjean, "the expression on a menhir's face changes with the light."

Generally speaking, menhirs are massive and often the sculptor expresses realism with clearly defined shoulders. The limbs play a secondary role as, in all, there are only six menhirs with arms and there are never any legs. The eyes and an open mouth are frequently incised, rather than shown with engraved lines, giving the impression that the statue is uttering a cry. The nose and chin stick out, and the ears are occasionally hinted at. There are a few menhirs with breasts but no sexual attributes. Some menhirs are armed with swords and daggers, and have some clothing or protective armor. Sculptors limited the carving of the back of the menhir to a rounded nape of the neck, the backbone, the ribs, and the shoulder blades.

One day, while I was visiting the prehistoric site, Grosjean pointed to the head of a menhir and exclaimed, "What a masterpiece of prehistoric art, what a noble head he has, what virility in the expression!" Charles-Antoine Cesari, on whose land the Filitosa statues stand, replied, "Oh, I don't know, I think that's the head of a woman." Grosjean retorted, "It's a man of granite with female hormones."

The Castaldu menhir has what appear to be breasts, which has led some experts to consider it a woman warrior. But Leandri thinks it would be wiser to believe it was armor with prominent pectorals, like those of Bronze Age warriors.

The two menhir statues in Cauria, each roughly nine feet high, are among the most detailed sculptures on the island. Their silhouettes, says Leandri, are phallic. Their faces in relief are clearly visible at midday in the best lighting conditions. The Corsican prehistoric sculptor or, more accurately, an indigenous artist on an island that became Corsica three millennia later, accentuated the realism of his menhirs by sculpting their arms and their hands.

One of the most magnificent monuments, in Leandri's view, is the "very beautiful menhir of Santa Maria. With its imposing mass and fine appearance, the Santa Maria menhir is unquestionably one of the masterpieces of Megalithic statuary. The face is realistic and quite clearly sculpted. The ears protrude slightly," he says.

Franck Leandri, one of only two official French Ministry of Culture staff archeologists on the island, doesn't believe in seeing, as Grosjean did, "a clear individual in every menhir. Let's just say that they are often extraordinary works of art in the early days of humanity and they stand in splendid settings of sea and rugged mountains. You find menhirs on mountain passes, at river crossings and at crossroads, and at the source of rivers and streams and springs. The views from them are stunning. No wonder Corsica is called the 'île de beauté.'"

On seeing a menhir for the first time, one is inclined to take it for granite. A mistake. Prehistoric artists also sculpted, but not so frequently, in schist, limestone and sandstone.

Near Filitosa, in a meadow full of poppies, lilies, wild mauve flowers and haystacks, shaded by a 500-year-old olive tree and ringed by 6,000-foot mountains, stand five tall menhirs. It is one of these that looks like George Washington. Another, viewed from the side, has a graceful serpentine movement. It will take more than vandalizing tourists and a Cesari mare who likes to rub her head on the menhir faces to damage these early monumental statues of Western art. No disrespectful visitor can inscribe a graffito on a menhir because the granite is unresponsive.

Although the menhirs have been around for thousands of years, and although the French are very keen on their prehistoric paintings at Lascaux, Les Eyzies and the southwest, it was not until 1838 that anyone thought of finding and counting menhirs. That year the writer Prosper Merimée rode a horse around the island's difficult mountainous roads, paths and goat trails to take a census of the ancient monuments. Actually, he found surprisingly few.

More than a century passed before another "continental," as Corsicans call the mainland French, got interested in menhirs. That was Roger Grosjean, a Parisian son of a judge who wanted him to become a lawyer. Roger dutifully studied law but his heart was set on flying. On the eve of World War II he became one of the country's youngest fighter-pilots. Indirectly, this led Grosjean to archeology and to becoming the pioneer of Corsican prehistoric research. It happened in a roundabout way.

A German pursuit plane shot down Grosjean's aircraft over Provence in the south of France. A crash landing in a forest broke his plane into hundreds of pieces, while Grosjean himself stayed in one piece and spent a year in a hospital. Escaping to London via Spain and Portugal, he was trained in England to detect camouflaged German V-1 launching ramps in occupied northern France, and this led to archeology. For the training flights consisted of finding and photographing archeological sites in the English countryside for the benefit of British scientists who went on digging throughout the war.

"One day I took a jeep to visit one of the excavations," recalled Grosjean. "I loved what I saw and I said to myself I'm going to become an archeologist." He did. Aged 26, Grosjean studied prehistory seriously at the Sorbonne and the prestigious Collège de France. From the outset he was interested in Corsica even though "everyone said it wasn't worth digging there because there was nothing to dig up."

"But," Grosjean asked himself, "why should this large, centrally-located Mediterranean island be so poor in prehistoric vestiges when all around it, in neighboring Sardinia, Italy, southern France, and Spain, the earth yielded such a rich crop of monuments for prehistorians? Why, in Sardinia alone, just a few miles south of Corsica, there were 7,000 large stone monuments."

But Grosjean remained discreet about his interest in Corsican menhirs. He didn't want this virgin territory stolen from him by other archeologists. With the help of a shepherd, Charles-Antoine Cesari, the great, great grandson of Merimée's shepherd-guide, he prospected on a 160-foot hillock not far from the sea. There in Filitosa he made his first important discovery. Embedded in the wall of what he judged to be a religious edifice, he found menhirs hacked into three or four pieces.

"They had clearly sculptured heads," said Grosjean. Leandri agreed they did. Yet 19th century "students" described the few menhirs with which they were familiar as "very crudely sculptured." Grosjean looked at them carefully and said, "On the contrary, they were finely sculptured works of art. No one had taken the trouble to have a good look at them."

Unfortunately, Roger Grosjean died at the early age of 55 in 1975, but not before he had unearthed the island's principal Bronze Age sites and 40 of the 100 menhir statues identified in 2004.

"Corsica is a marvelous outdoor museum," said Grosjean. "While Filitosa is the most impressive collection of menhirs, it is by no means the only site. There are at least half a dozen important ensembles of menhir statues in southern Corsica around Porto Vecchio, Bonifacio, Levie and Cauria, as well as handsome isolated menhirs scattered throughout the island. At Pagliaiu, near Sartène, there are two rows of some 50 menhirs (but only three sculptured ones), stretching north-south and facing east."

Grosjean said, "There are enough buried and concealed menhirs to keep 10 full-time archeologists busy excavating for the next 200 years." Even allowing for his enthusiasm and possible exaggeration, Corsica's menhirs have become a leading tourist attraction and a major commercial enterprise.

Filitosa's group of 17 is the most popular site. Every year between 150,000 and 200,000 visitors each pay about 4 euros or over $5 to walk around the fenced-in site and gaze at menhirs.

The attitude of islanders toward menhirs has changed radically. In the past Corsicans destroyed them through ignorance and while vainly looking for treasures. When they came to realize that these monuments were the works of art of their very distant ancestors, they started finding and protecting them with their shotguns. On one occasion when a forest fire broke out near one major site, Corsicans who had exchanged fewer words than shots with each other in 10 years rushed to the rescue of the menhirs with water buckets.

One islander remarked to me at Filitosa: "Menhirs are the best thing that has happened to Corsica since Napoleon." Or, as the island's numerous anti-Bonapartists would say, "including Napoleon."

If the menhirs are as important as claimed, why then did no other archeologists or art historians or André Malraux, when he was Minister of Culture under Charles de Gaulle, get excited and start digging? One possible explanation is that Corsica is very underdeveloped, surprisingly unexplored, a mountainous island with tortuous roads. Only recently have the continental French found Corsica interesting, essentially for basking in the sun along its long, beautiful coast. Before Napoleon, and since, Corsica has been discriminated against economically by the mainland and abandoned to its inhabitants, the most energetic and best educated of whom have "emigrated" to Paris, Marseilles and the Midi (southern France). It took a Parisian like Roger Grosjean to disregard the old belief that Corsica had no prehistory and to do something about it.

How well have the menhirs survived the passage of three millennia? Surprisingly well, considering the inevitable erosion due to rain, sun, storms . . . . and vandalism. Four years ago, though, someone actually stole a menhir statue, weighing about a ton, which had been unearthed and excavated in five fragmented pieces by Franck Leandri in the Nebbiu region of northeastern Corsica, just south of Cap Corse near Bastia. The thieves (there must have been more than one!) have never been found, nor has any trace of the monument.

No wonder Leandri is not impressed by the safety precautions surrounding the menhirs. The "owners" of the menhirs are the farmers and landholders on whose property they stand. They can't sell or dispose of them in any way, but they are not obliged to take special care of them. "I know one 'owner,'" says Leandri, "who dusts off his menhir's face with a dog brush!"

Discovered in one place, menhirs have often been transplanted to a more visible location. In 1965, the U Nativo menhir was unearthed near a stream and a low mountain pass. Although fragmented, this more than seven-feet-long limestone monument was repaired, reconstituted and moved to the main square of the town of Patrimonio where it stands today.

The first menhir to be recognized in 1840 by Prosper Merimée, the Apriciani, was found in Sagone in west-central Corsica and first transported to a place in front of the Cathedral of Sant' Appiano. Recently it was moved again, this time to the entrance to the village of Vico. "Without any guarantee of its safe-keeping," comments Leandri.

Yet another menhir, unearthed in the small valley of Bulbia in 1993, was moved by its discoverer to his land on the heights of Cargese in western Corsica. This menhir bears the intriguing name of U Scumunicatuu, meaning the Excommunicated. The name seems to suggest either secret beliefs or reflect the Catholic Church's condemnation of worshippers of stone and wooden idols. In the Middle Ages, menhir sites were considered pagan. Mind you, in one menhir at Pagliaiu, erosion dug a hole in the granite and the water accumulating in it was thought to have magic virtues.

I asked the 39-year-old Corsican archeologist how these unique works of art from the dawn of humanity could be protected from the elements, the looters, from careless or irresponsible proprietors. He answered immediately: "Put them all in a museum. There they would be safe, well looked after, and accessible at a reasonable price to everyone—tourists, art historians, archeologists, Corsicans. What a beautiful collection the island's 100 menhirs would make!

"But such a sensible solution is not for tomorrow or next year. There is no will-power in government circles in Paris or Ajaccio to force private owners of most of the island's menhirs (roughly 90%) to hand them over, even with compensation, to museums. There is an obvious conflict between the conservation of menhirs and their touristic exploitation."

At present, Leandri points out, there are only two full-time, paid archeologists (by the Ministry of Culture) on the entire island, himself and his director, Joseph Cesari, to look after and protect Corsica's prehistoric monuments. This compares with 300 to 400 full-time "diggers" in the much more "backward" nearby island of Sardinia. The Italians have built two large archeological museums there, making Corsica look pitiful and outclassed.

"De Gaulle liked to speak about 'la grandeur de la France.' But viewed from Corsica," Leandri says, "it's more like 'les illusions de grandeur.'"

Investigating the Extinction of
Tyrannosaurus Ress

Not so many years ago one could count the number of dinosaur eggs that had been dug up in Mongolia and the Dakotas on one hand. Had they not been fossilized, they'd have made a large omelet.

Then Raymond Dughi, the curator of the Museum of Natural History in the southern French city of Aix-en-Provence, discovered an entire cemetery of dinosaur eggs, hundreds, perhaps thousands of them. Many of them, of every size and shape, some resembling a football, lay barely buried in the red clay earth beneath the Mont Sainte Victoire in Provence, a mountain immortalized by Cézanne in many paintings. Dughi immortalized the dinosaur egg cemetery for fellow paleontologists.

At first Dughi told no one about his extraordinary discovery. He took several eggs back to his laboratory in Aix-en-Provence to examine the shells. His plan was to try to come up with an explanation for the sudden disappearance of dinosaurs from the earth. Meanwhile, a local schoolteacher had unearthed a dinosaur egg in her garden. As she was likely to report her find to an eminent paleontologist in Paris, Dughi saw himself about to be deprived of his scientific "scoop." So he hastened to submit numerous reports and papers describing his find to the Academy of Science. This insured his fame.

It also attracted any reporter who followed communications to the Academy. I did and went to Aix and persuaded Dughi to show me "his" cemetery of dinosaur eggs. My credibility was clearly established when I pointed out that Tyrannosaurus Ress was my ancestor. Admittedly not a direct line as it was interrupted by Oedipus Ress. In any event the sight of such a huge number of dinosaur eggs overwhelmed me.

"If I were you," I urged Dughi, "I'd have the name of your city changed to 'Eggs-en-Provence.'"

Several weeks later I received a call from a former colleague on the Paris Herald, Roy McMullen. "I see you've been in Aix-en-Provence lately," he said. "How do you know?" I asked, since I had not yet written anything about it. McMullen explained, "I saw an article in Le Monde by a French reporter who had gone to Aix to see the cemetery. Raymond Dughi told him that he was not the first journalist to visit. There had been an American reporter who had suggested changing the name of the city to Eggs-en-Provence. It was obvious to me that only you would make such a terrible pun."

Copy Paper

Dropping by a French daily's editorial room one evening, I heard a strange shout, "Pass me some beefsteak." And one reporter obliged by giving a colleague a handful of plain white paper. It was copy paper to be used for writing headlines for a story. At the time, I wasn't curious enough to ask how copy paper became to be known as "beefstek." Many years later, in a paperless electronic age, I started asking journalists for an explanation. No one had a clue. Finally I came across an elderly French reporter in Nairobi who did.

"Just after World War II," he explained, "there was a great shortage of paper. Well, when newspapers were printed, there was always some unused paper left on the rollers. The printers gave that extra white paper to nearby butchers who wrapped the meat they sold in it. And journalists began to call it their copy paper, beefstek."

In those days, a popular haunt of French reporters was the Left Bank, avant-garde cabaret, L'Ecluse.

Whatever the Traffic Will Bear or a Tail of Two Cities

One of the main reasons why I have stayed in Europe after working as a journalist and an international civil servant can be summed up in one word: dogs. In France and Switzerland you can go just about anywhere with your dog. Only hospitals are really off limits. In the United States, alas, there's hardly anywhere you can go with your dog, except the woods.

Now, Parisian dog-lovers, with some reason, believe that their city is the world's doggiest. After all, dogs are to be found just about everywhere, especially in restaurants. As Art Buchwald observed several decades ago, poodles eat from the plates of their mistresses. Little wonder that doggie bags are seldom seen in Paris.

I have lived in Paris with two boxers and in Geneva with three bearded collies. I can assure Parisians, and American dog-lovers, that Geneva is the doggier of the two cities. Here, in Calvin's supposedly strict and austere citadel, dogs not only dine out and frequent airports, railroad stations, department stores, fashionable shops, bars, restaurants, trolley cars and trains, they occasionally make it into church (Protestant and Catholic). Indeed, dogs are deemed worthy enough to pay full fare on buses and tramways, whatever their age and size, while senior citizens go for half-fare.

What is more impressive—admittedly only for Geneva's dog-lovers—dogs can go to the movies. My first beardie, Sophie, went to half a dozen cinemas, and not to see "Faithful Lassie" or "The Call of the Wild." She was an adult dog with mature if unexpected tastes. "Cyrano de Bergerac," for example, left her cold (or, rather, sleeping), but the fine Danish film, "Babette's Feast," based on Isak Dinesen's story, had her watching intently.

When I planned to take Sophie to dinner and then to the movies, I telephoned the cinema. After asking an anodyne question, like "When does the film end?", I'd inquire: "Do you mind if I come with a well-behaved, middle-sized dog?" The answer was invariably, "Just a second." After consultation the ticket seller would say, "No, but if your dog barks . . ." "Yes," I'd interrupt, "if my dog barks, we'll both be leaving because it's not a good film."

One evening we lined up to buy a ticket for "Babette's Feast." A little girl in front of me asked me if dogs could go to the movies. "How old are you?" I asked. "Nine." "Well, Sophie is older than you, and if you can go, so can she." The girl was unconvinced. "Does she pay?" "No." "Do you pay for her?" "No."

When the film was over, Sophie and I walked to our car. "Look, Mommy," said the little girl, "there's the dog that saw the same film as we did." Then she asked me, "Did your dog like the film?" "Oh, yes, very much so," I replied, "but I think actually she preferred the book."

One might expect Calvinist Geneva not to be so freethinking in its attitude to dogs. But I have found other European cities equally unpredictable in their outlook. Recently, on a trip to Bulgaria, I discovered that compared to Sofia, even Geneva is conventional. Consider the facts.

I was being shown around Sofia on foot by Vessalin Seykov, a veteran reporter with the Bulgarian Telegraph Agency (BTA). At the end of the day Seykov said, "We're now too close to your hotel for taxi drivers to want to take you there, and we're too far to walk so we'll take a trolley car."

There was no queue for the tramway, but I noticed a tall hirsute traveler waiting a few yards away. He was standing on his hind paws, attached to the man beside him by a rather fragile leash. The huge brown bear looked eight or nine feet tall but may have been no bigger than your ordinary professional basketball player.

"Is he planning to take the same tramway as we are?" I asked.

"Of course not," snorted Seykov. "We don't even allow dogs on tramways."

We got on the first section of the two-car, Swiss-made trolley. "He got on, too," I said, pointing to the bear in the adjoining car.

"Nonsense," Seykov insisted, "bears are not permitted on public transport in Bulgaria."

"Maybe not," I agreed, "but just look down the aisle and you'll see that bear."

By this time the bear was on all four paws, looking out the window from the rear platform. Most of the travelers had vacated a large area around him. His were not the paws that refresh. Two young lovers, however, more fascinated by one another than fearful of bears, were entwined around a tramway pole and each other, oblivious of their unusual fellow traveler a few feet away.

"Geneva buses charge me half-fare as a senior citizen," I remarked. "Do you think that the bear pays half-fare as a senior bear, or full fare like my old shaggy dog?"

"I doubt that the ticket collector will check his ticket," Seykov replied.

"Not that I long for the old regime," he added, "but at least there was some order and authority then. A bear could not have hopped onto a trolley in the old days."

We stared out the window for several stops. The bear was still there.

"I don't think I'll tell my wife about the bear," Seykov murmured. "She'd think I had stopped at a pub on the way home and had too many drinks."

Pablo and the Other Painter

One balmy evening Pablo and Jacqueline Picasso were dining with two friends on the terrace of his favorite restaurant in Cannes, Félix, when an itinerant artist came by. "May I do your portrait, Madame?" he said to Picasso's wife. Annoyed, she snapped, "Merci, c'est déjà fait" (Thank you, it has already been done).

The spurned painter entered Félix's to look for a customer. Finding none, he headed for the door. This time, on the terrace, he spotted Picasso. "Pablo!" he exclaimed. Picasso stood up, smiled and the two men embraced. A long animated conversation followed. An embarrassed Jacqueline sat silently. When the itinerant artist said "au revoir" to everyone, she said to her husband, "I didn't know he was a good friend of yours, Pablo, or I wouldn't have been so unkind to him. Why didn't you tell me?"

To which Pablo replied, "Jacqueline, I never saw him before in my life."

*   *   *

Harmonious Jingling Upon Words

No egrets whatsoever—Egrets only

Trouble with salade niçoise is that there's an embarrass d'anchoix

Stopping a friend whistling off key—you're a whistler only a mother could love

Seeking a modus vivaldi

What's Chile's (unfavorite) wine? Pinochet Noir

As the botanist says, with friends like that, who needs anemones?

A Cultural Pilgrimage with a Donkey

Exactly 128 years ago, on September 22, 1878, Robert Louis Stevenson set out with a donkey on a mountain promenade in the Massif Central of south-central France. They walked about 120 miles in 12 days. A year later Stevenson published a short account of the journey, "Travels with a Donkey in the Cévennes."

Most travel books are soon forgotten. At best they make armchair readers dream in comfort. Not so Stevenson's "Travels with a Donkey." Not only is the delightful book considered today a classic of travel writing in the English-speaking world, but it continues, well over a century later, to induce readers to make the difficult trip themselves. Indeed, in the past 55 years Stevenson's book has created a literary cult.

On foot, preferably with, but sometimes without a donkey, on horseback, in trailers and automobiles, Stevensonians make the pilgrimage from the small town of Le Monastier, near Le Puy, over 4,000- and 5,000-foot peaks to the "Camisard" (southern French Protestant) center of St. Jean-du-Gard. Invariably, like Stevenson, they halt at the Trappist monastery of Notre Dame des Neiges (Our Lady of the Snows).

The literary pilgrims come from all over the Anglo-Saxon world, from the highlands of Scotland to down under in New Zealand. Oddly, each one thinks that he or she is the first to have had the idea. An American woman loved the region so much after the trip that she settled for several years in Le Monastier, and offered the town a marble plaque commemorating Stevenson's journey with his donkey, Modestine. A Welsh university student wrote a term paper about it after also making the trip with a donkey.

Describing the reaction of townspeople to his proposed donkey trip, Stevenson wrote: "A traveller of my sort was a thing hitherto unheard of in that district. I was looked upon with contempt, like a man who should project a journey to the moon" (sic).

Curiously, 71 years were to pass before a slight young Englishwoman named Vera Singer launched the Stevensonian donkey travel cult. In 1949 Ms. Singer turned up in Le Monastier with just enough money to buy a donkey, re-baptized, of course, Modestine II. If Stevenson paid about $30 and a glass of brandy for his "diminutive she-ass, not much bigger than a dog, the colour of a mouse, with a kindly eye and a determined under-jaw . . . . [and] a Quakerish elegance," Vera Singer was obliged to spend $58 for her traveling companion.

By 1964 the inflation in Monasterian donkeys was such that the Welshman, Andrew Evans, was asked $150 for one, and reluctantly paid $80. In 1969 the going price had risen to $100.

Now Stevenson's account of his journey was anything but a precise geographical explanation of how to walk from one point to another. He got lost and so do most pilgrims. Vera Singer nearly froze to death one night some 5,500 feet up on Mont Lozère and had to be rescued by French firemen.

Right on Vera's heels came a New Zealander remembered only as "Monsieur White." He said he planned to write a book about his journey. No one knows if he ever did, but he left imperishable traces of his trek in the form of two sepia postcards for tourists, which show him leading Modestine III.

Clifford Fowkes of Edinburgh made more of an impression on the French of the region in 1967 by doing the entire trip dressed in a kilt. Even Stevenson was not that much of a Scotsman.

That same year a newly-wed couple, Michael and Jill Elliot, arrived in Le Monastier intending to spend their honeymoon retracing Stevenson's steps in the company of a donkey. Somehow this strange manège-à-trois never did get going.

Then there were two Oxford University students, John Bowder and Diana Gilbert. After five hours, they had advanced only two miles. Their donkey adamantly refused to cross the Pont de l'Estaing over the Gazeille River. It turned out that the donkey was allergic to bridges. Once a Le Monastier cattle dealer had trucked him across this and another bridge over the Loire, the donkey moved forward at a decent pace, that is to say, like Stevenson's Modestine, he made two or two-and-a-half miles an hour.

One summer some Americans named Richardson showed up, bought three donkeys and formed a caravan. Townspeople were impressed until the Richardsons ridiculed themselves by riding out of town on their donkeys. They were damned with faint brays. A picture of them riding donkeyback adds a hilarious note to a permanent Stevenson donkey cult exhibition in the town hall.

An English kindergarten principal from Somerset, Jane Tarr, enjoyed her pilgrimage in an automobile so much that she returned with her husband the following year to repeat it on foot. "What an unspoilt village Le Monastier is," she remarked. "It's still just as Stevenson described it."

Undoubtedly the most enthusiastic of the literary pilgrims were the Gladstones from Berkeley, California. "I had read Stevenson's book as a young girl," Betty Gladstone recalled, "and I always wanted to take the same trip."

Her daughters, Roberta and Carol, who were aged 18 and 12 at the time, gleefully went along.

The Gladstones' Modestine was delivered in a Citroën 2CV, a car which appears to be a product of Continental Can. She weighed a mere 300 pounds and, after collapsing every hour or so on the first two days, finally consented to carry a load of 120 lbs. "We were terribly discouraged in the beginning," said Betty, "and we talked about giving up. Then the reporter of a regional newspaper interviewed us walking along the road and praised our courage and toughness, so we decided we couldn't quit."

The Gladstones preferred the month of May to Stevenson's month of September. It was a poor choice, at least that year. "Halfway, we got caught in a snowstorm high up in the Cévennes," said Ms. Gladstone. "Another day there was a terrific hailstorm. Then the weather turned torrid and we felt as if we were crossing a desert. One night we got lost in a forest."

Notwithstanding, the Gladstones reached St. Jean-du-Gard in 13 days, only 24 hours off Stevenson's pace. "It poured so hard one day," she explained apologetically, "that we just stayed put all day long in a hayloft."

There were happy moments and annoying ones on the journey. Children lined village streets to cheer them on, but one day in a downpour gendarmes provoked the Gladstones' indignation by insisting they show them their passports.

"The scenery, especially in the Cévennes, was absolutely superb," said Betty, "and we were never depressed."

Shortly after the journey the Gladstones moved to Le Monastier where they lived all year round for three years.

While they were there, they met two fellow Californians, a retired, elderly couple, Charles and Carolyn Planck, who were no longer up to doing the trip with a donkey, but did make it in a Volkswagen camper.

Not all pilgrims contact local authorities. As a rule, only those in search of a donkey do. Recently an American woman rode the Stevenson itinerary on a horse, but never identified herself to anyone.

When one stops to think about it, few if any books written more than a century ago, or for that matter last year, have such a galvanizing effect on people today. It certainly seemed worthwhile trying to discover why. In this do-it-yourself age, clearly the only way to go about it was to acquire a donkey and to start walking. I did and haven't had so much fun in donkeys' years.

Although Modestine put Le Monastier on the map, at any rate the literary map of the Anglo-Saxon world, there wasn't a donkey to be had in this town of 1,245 souls when Pierre Honegger, a Time Magazine photographer, and I looked for one in 1969. Happily, Le Monastier possessed a procurer of donkeys par excellence in the person of Renée Robert, a retired schoolteacher and Stevenson lover.

Madame Robert led us at once to a meadow in the nearby mountain hamlet of Châteauneuf. There we encountered Bijou, a frisky, three-year-old, gray and golden-brown donkey with white patches. Substantially bigger than Stevenson's or anyone else's Modestine, Bijou weighed well over 600 pounds.

Sitting at a sidewalk café in the pastis-filtered sunlight of Le Monastier, I asked Bijou's owner, Joseph Habouzit, what he would sell or rent the animal for. Monsieur Habouzit preferred a rental arrangement. We don't rent donkeys every day, I explained, so what would be a reasonable price? He had no idea, so we proposed the rate for a small rented car, a Citroën 2CV—$7 a day. Habouzit readily agreed and said that for that price we would be getting an American donkey, or anyway one "whose ancestors came from the Americas."

As we planned to depart the next morning from the post office square, near the Stevenson memorial plaque, Bijou would require overnight lodging. That problem was solved by a cattle dealer named Ernest Charre who used his stable as a "pension" for Stevenson cult donkeys.

For the sum of $30 we acquired a packsaddle from Henri Giraud, a craftsman whose great grandfather, Father Adam, sold Modestine to the writer. His ancestry was more impressive than his craftsmanship. Like Stevenson, we had nothing but trouble and dissatisfaction with the saddle. It whirled around Bijou's belly and back with the speed of a revolving door. It wouldn't stay put. I improvised a saddle-packing arrangement with a potato sack and cord.

On the eve of our departure our path crossed with a first-year Cambridge University medical student from Chester, Richard Kupfer. He had arrived in Le Monastier a few days earlier, thinking he was the first Englishmen to discover the out-of-the-way mountain town. He had spotted the Stevenson memorial and thought it would be nice to make the trip, too. We joined forces. Three men did not prove one too many for Bijou.

Mayor Charles Convers put on his tri-color sash to see us off properly. A small crowd gathered, more inclined to jeer than to cheer. In Stevenson's own words, we "went forth from the stable door as an ox goeth to the slaughter." Bijou ambled forward about 20 yards, then lay down to protest and contest. He started rolling over on his back, squashing our picnic peaches before we could push him right side up.

Unlike all donkey walkers since Stevenson, according to Madame Robert, we did not take the asphalt road out of town but struck cross-country down a fairly steep, rocky hill. For the next three days and 30-odd miles we crossed fields and swamps and streams, avoiding even country lanes whenever possible. Photographer Honegger guided our team with a Swiss army compass (he was Swiss) and a French military map with a one-to-50,000 scale but without a grid square.

Bijou determined the speed of our walk. Despite a hay-filled night, he was hungry. Every minute or two he stooped to munch. When he wasn't eating delicious thistles, he was trying to nibble at us. Once he got a pretty fair bite of Richard's hand. Our sentimentality about domestic animals suddenly excluded donkeys and, like Stevenson, Richard equipped himself with a goad that impressed Bijou for the remainder of the journey.

Bijou's eating habits were contagious. No, not for thistles, but after the 50th halt in a barley field, the young Englishman tried a stalk himself. "Super," said he.

We discovered, as the Welsh pilgrim Andrew Evans remarked, that "the presence of a donkey opened the hearts of more than one person" toward us. Bijou was, if nothing else, a conversation piece. "You're following in Stevenson's traces, aren't you?" remarked a peasant woman. "Well, you're not the first, you know. Every year we see several foreigners pass with a donkey."

When Bijou and an army of gnats permitted, we admired the landscape, surely the principal reason for Stevenson and latter-day disciples to make the journey. The broad, stony path ran straight like a Roman road between "fences" of volcanic rocks. Beyond them lay yellow and green fields, red brown soil, and above them a few miles away the extinct volcanoes of the Massif Central. An expert at distinguishing between venomous and non-poisonous mushrooms would have found dinner at his feet. Had there been a late summer sun the glades of Scottish pines would have invited a halt.

We had succeeded fairly well in keeping our feet dry when we came to our first stream. Too broad to be jumped in one hop, it had stones that formed a bridge. Bijou balked at wading across. "Get ready for a possible photo," I said to Pierre Honegger who stationed himself on the opposite bank. Holding on to his rope bridle, I jumped onto the first stone, hoping to set Bijou an example he would follow. He didn't and I landed in the river. Pierre fell over backwards laughing and didn't take the picture. "Don't count on me to do it again," I remarked. Bijou promptly waded across.

In very little time Bijou objected strenuously to carrying the potato sack. So we took turns shouldering it. In the end we were loaded down like donkeys and Bijou strode along like a Stevenson lover carrying only a canteen, an empty one at that. After several hours of this farce, we dumped all but a knapsack at a café and made a deal for the proprietor to transport our gear to an inn at Le Bouchet-St.-Nicholas, Stevenson's first stop, and ours as well.

We were still a long distance from Le Bouchet when darkness fell. It was raining hard and the meadows though which we had to pass were a muddy pond. Foolishly, we had left our flashlight in our potato sack, and we wallowed slowly ahead. We came face to face with a stone wall. Bijou refused to budge. He had climbed much steeper mounds, but he would have nothing to do with a stone wall. So we removed the heavy stones one by one. We left enough room for all of Hannibal's elephants to pass through it, but Bijou wasn't interested. We pushed and pulled and goaded and shouted. Remembering Stevenson's magic word "proot," which worked so well with Modestine, we prooted. As Stevenson wrote, we "prooted like a lion, prooted mellifluously like a sucking-dove, but Modestine would be neither softened nor intimidated." Nor was Bijou. We gave up and spent half an hour before finding a way out of the field.

At 8:30 at night we stumbled, soaking wet, into the Café de la Poste at Le Bouchet-St.-Nicholas. "We've got accommodation and hay for your donkey," said the innkeeper, "but neither food nor a room for you."

The hospitality of a neighboring village left something to be desired since we were offered a room and dinner, providing we ate at once in our drenched clothes. We did, while swearing about French hostelry.

Next morning we found Bijou somewhat unhappy, his waterlogged rope bridle touched his eyes and was so stiff that the Gordian knots had to be cut with a knife. Bijou walked into a game of "pétanque" (a French variety of bowling) near his stable, scattering the players. One of them said he was "un expert en âne" (a donkey expert), and he removed the rope altogether. Bijou was free and wasted no time running after his tormentors of the previous day. As we zigzagged around the muddy square, the villagers laughed their heads off. Finally, the "expert" caught Bijou and put on a new and better bridle.

"That's worth at least an apéritif, isn't it?" he suggested. We bought him two on the spot and left the café with a week's charge account for him.

Another day's stroll left us comfortably lodged, but Bijou in a stable two miles off in the country. Monday dawned rainy and, thinking to save time and an extra hour's two-mile walk in the rain, we hired a man in Langogne to transport our beast-of-no-burden in his small Peugeot station wagon.

"I transport my own donkey from one county fair to another," he said confidently, "so I'll have no trouble with your donkey." An hour later we were driving at a snail's pace with Bijou taking his time walking behind the car. No amount of pushing or threatening or prooting had persuaded him to get into the Peugeot.

"Wait until I get half a dozen of my buddies to help me," swore the donkey transporter. "We'll make him get in."

When six people pushing and pulling failed to make Bijou come through the rear door, it was decided to drag him in through one of the side doors. While six chaps pulled on his rope, one man pushed perilously from the rear and another courageous fellow collapsed Bijou's front legs. Finally, they succeeded in shoving and choking the poor animal into the right side door. But Bijou kept right on going and leaped outside through the open left door.

By afternoon we had passed through a forest of birches and beeches and reached the Trappist monastery of Notre Dame des Neiges where Stevenson, the unbelieving Protestant, got into hot arguments with sectarian Catholics, and to which he devotes the longest section of his book.

If there is anyone between Le Monastier and St. Jean-du-Gard who is familiar with Robert Louis Stevenson's book and the literary cult it provoked, it is the monks of Notre Dame des Neiges. As we entered the monastery grounds leading Bijou, a talkative Trappist monk, that is, talkative for a Trappist, came to greet us. Upon spotting the donkey, he uttered one word, "Stevenson?"

We introduced ourselves to Father Zephyrin, the keeper of the monastery stables. "He is a particularly handsome donkey," he said "but his ears are an inch-and-a-half too short for a donkey of his size. I'll put him in the same stable where Modestine stayed and give him some hay."

We then met Father Albert, the beekeeper and an amateur historian. He, too, said "Stevenson? There have been quite a few Stevenson pilgrims with donkeys here this year. You're probably the last ones because the weather has turned bad. Do you plan to go another nine days in Stevenson's footsteps? No, you're stopping here? And sending the donkey back home to Le Monastier? Well, that's cheating a bit, but it sounds like a sensible idea."

After only three days of walking with Bijou, we wondered whether Stevenson's only mistake was not to have called his book "Travails with a Donkey."

In any event, far from dying out, the donkey walk has become increasingly popular, according to the Le Monastier Tourist Office Director, David Sascani. Three French paperback translations of Stevenson's book have appeared lately, and the French have now begun to make the pilgrimage. In an average year 40 or 50 literary pilgrims turn up to ask for help in finding a donkey, says Monsieur Sascani, who directs them to Marcel Exbrayat. Monsieur Exbrayat runs a rent-a-donkey business from his farm. (I think that the "bray" in his name is coincidental.) Inflation has affected the donkey business, too. The day rate for renting a donkey in the Cévennes is 35 euros or about $43. If you do the entire trip in Stevensonian time, i.e., 12 days, it will set you back around $500, plus the hay.

A Really Good Coffee

The English editor of the bilingual magazine, "Réalités," was looking for a translator of an article about life on the Argentine Pampas. Even someone whose mother tongue was Spanish might not be familiar with the Argentine terms. How to understand and to translate the text into English?

"Telephone the press attaché of the Argentine Embassy," I was advised. "He'll translate everything for you, but be warned, he's passionate about coffee, and at whatever hour you turn up to see him, he will offer you coffee. You must say 'yes,' and make a fuss about its taste."

I took the advice and arrived at the embassy at 11 in the morning. It was not, I thought, a propitious hour for an apéritif or, for that matter, a cup of coffee.

The press attaché looked at the article and said, "That's very easy, but before we start, wouldn't you like some coffee?"

"Oh, yes," I said enthusiastically. He pushed a button, a valet dressed in an 18th century costume appeared and, minutes later, reappeared with an elegant silver coffee service and beautiful porcelain cups.

I sipped the coffee as if it were a 1937 Vosne Romanée.

"Do you Argentines, like us North Americans, buy your coffee in Colombia or Venezuela or Brazil?" I inquired cautiously.

"Why do you ask?"

"Because," I replied, "this is undoubtedly the finest coffee I have drunk."

"I am delighted to hear you say so," said the diplomat, "because it's Nescafé."

Nothing Vile about this Canard

Probably no Paris journalists are as handsomely paid as those on "Le Canard Enchainé," a satirical, non-conformist, anti-clerical, leftwing weekly. It takes no advertising, enjoys a very large circulation (400,000) and makes a lot of money. The Enchained Duck was born on September 10, 1915 in the middle of World War I. In view of the nervousness of the American media and its fear of being accused of being unpatriotic in respect to the war in Iraq, it is very interesting to see how the French journal covered the first world war.

"Everyone knows that since the start of the war the French press without any exception has communicated to its readers only implacably true news," said Le Canard Enchainé in its first issue. "Eh bien, the public is fed up with this. The public wants false news for a change. It will get them. To achieve this pretty result, the editors of the Canard Enchainé, recoiling before no sacrifice, have unhesitatingly signed a one-year contract with the famous Wolff Press Agency in Berlin which will transmit every week all the false news of the entire world by special barbed wire."

While shells exploded and patriotic censors' scissor fingers itched, the Canard's editorial "Coin, coin, coin" (the sound of a quacking duck) went on: "We give our word not to surrender to the deplorable mania of the day, that is, to publish under any pretext a strategic, diplomatic or economic article. Besides, its small format makes this sort of bad joke impossible. We shall insert, after minute verification, only rigorously inexact news. In these conditions we do not doubt for a second that the vast public will give us a hearty welcome. In this hope we extend to the public our condolences."

There was hardly a less auspicious moment than the second year of World War I for the appearance of an anti-militarist, anti-conformist, satirical periodical. Nevertheless, the four-page, 10-centime "journal humoristique" caught on.

The first issues contained some ferocious humor. In a Paris-datelined dispatch from Wolff in Berlin (Wolff was the official German news agency of the day), under the headline "The Air War, 10 Zeppelins over Paris, Tragic and Comic Scenes," the paper wrote: "Ten Zeppelins flew over Paris from 10 p.m. to 4 a.m., and dropped 4,000 bombs in different parts of the capital. In the Belleville quarter it is no exaggeration to estimate the dead and wounded at 150,000. We must congratulate ourselves all the more since most of the victims were women and children."

Mixing black humor with Grouchoesque slapstick, another Wolff dispatch from Constantinople declared: "In the Dardanelles the cannons of forts, aided by two fishing smacks of the Ottoman fleet, victoriously halted the advance of the French-British squadron. Twenty-five French cruisers and 18 English dreadnoughts (maybe 19) were sunk by rifle fire at the entry to the straits. As a result, the waters of the Sea of Marmora, encountering this unexpected dam, are having great difficulty following their normal course. German-Turkish authorities have immediately adopted all necessary precautions against eventual floods. Ottoman subjects are begged to temporarily transport their villas to the interior. Allah is great and Von der Goltz is his prophet."

A forerunner of its mocking anti-clericalism was the quoted comment of a Paris worker upon seeing a high dignitary of the church emerge from the Basilica of Saint Denis in a magnificent scarlet robe, "Get a load of that lobster!"

The Canard's cartoons were just as biting as its dispatches. One showed a peasant mother trying to teach her baby to take his first steps as a soldier with a knotted stick limps by. The patriotic mother says to her baby, "If you don't want to learn to walk, you will never be able to go to the trenches like Monsieur."

Another popular Canard cartoon had a fur-coated rich woman and her curvaceous maid in a very low décolleté, standing in front of the master's bed. Says the maid: "Monsieur had only an hour furlough. Monsieur didn't have the time to wait for Madame."

Just how far the Canard could and did go is evident from the "Pater Noster du Poilu" (the soldier's Lord's Prayer) printed next to a picture of Marshal Joffre. It goes this way: "Our Joffre who art in Hell, Hallowed be thy name, Thy victory come, Thy will be done on earth as it is in the air. Give them this day their daily lead. Return the offensive to us as you have given it to those who have broken through. Lead us not to teutonization, But deliver us from the Boches. Amen." Editor Maurice Maréchal was finally silenced in 1915, but not for long. In 1916 he was back at it with the famous Baltimore submarine incident.

The French press reported that a German sub had sunk an allied vessel a few miles off the American coast, and wondered how the sub could have gotten there. Hastening to explain, the Canard indignantly denied that a German submarine could have crossed the Atlantic and revealed that "the truth is—and this is perfectly clear to any impartial, unprejudiced person—that the Boche submarine never crossed the ocean, but was assembled in Baltimore. Piece by piece, parbleu! It was simple, every piece was numbered. Then one day they removed the canvas and people shouted that a sub had arrived from Germany."

The Paris press, including the most serious dailies, promptly printed "reliable reports from very serious American contacts," without of course a reference to the Canard, that a German sub had been assembled in the United States, etc., etc.

The Canard gleefully rubbed their noses in the duck pond, commenting: "The stupidity of these great newspapers is so enormous that they fell upon this fable like a pig on a truffle. Yet we told you in our first issue that we would publish only false news. How more clearly can we say this? Why did these newspapers take us so seriously? After all, do we take their editors seriously?"

And to prove the point the Canard started publishing dispatches from "In Penguin Land from The Yearly Telegraph of London and The Time Is Money of Chicago."

Maréchal changed the name of his paper in 1919 to "Le Canard Déchainé," the Unchained Duck, but in 1920 he enchained the duck again and it is still Le Canard Enchaîné in 2006. However, it has doubled in size to eight pages and sells for 1.20 euros or about $1.40. The masthead notes that 2006 is the weekly's 91st year. Almost a centenarian.

Cheers! I Mean Kirs

When you drink a kir the next time, you might give a thought for whom the cocktail was named.

Yes, there was a man named Félix Kir, a quite extraordinary Frenchman of Alsatian background. He didn't invent the drink because the French, especially Burgundians, have been drinking this mixture of a dry white wine and cassis, a blackcurrant liqueur, for a long time.

But this Catholic priest, who appointed himself mayor of Dijon, popularized it so successfully that it became a familiar apéritif in sophisticated bars, cafes and restaurants all over the world.

Chanoine (Canon) Kir was a simple parish priest in Dijon when German troops entered the city. The socialist mayor fled. Like many Alsatians, Kir was a super French patriot so he walked into the city hall and sat down in the mayor's empty seat. As always, he was wearing a cassock.

A German colonel entered the mayor's office and approached Kir. "Heil Hitler!" he shouted. Kir just stared at him. "Heil Hitler!" the Wehrmacht officer repeated. Kir went on staring. Then the colonel stuck out his hand. Kir didn't budge. The colonel insisted, but Kir refused to shake his hand. When the German demanded an explanation for his rude behavior, Chanoine Kir replied calmly, "I never shake the hand of an officer below the rank of general."

That was just the beginning of the Nazi occupation army's problems with the cantankerous canon. Near Dijon there was the Longvic prisoner-of-war camp with 5,000 captured French soldiers. Working with the French resistance, the self-appointed mayor had thousands of counterfeit identity cards forged. Hundreds of POWs escaped.

Arrested once, then freed, he pursued his resistance activities. The Gestapo had enough. They arranged with a group of teenage French Fascists to shoot Kir. Four of them tracked him down to his modest flat in the handsome, semi-circular, 17th century "place" across from the town hall. The church-going sons of Kir's parishioners knew him well, of course, and he recognized them. One had a pistol.

Point-blank he shot five times at Kir, wounding him seriously, but sometimes missing him. Kir liked to point to dents in his stove where bullets hit.

"I counted five shots while I was lying on the floor," he told me during a visit to his little apartment. "I knew the sixth bullet would be the coup de grâce so I struggled up. Those Fascist kids thought they had killed me, so they were terrified when I appeared to rise from the dead. Instead of finishing me off, they fled. My resistance comrades rescued me."

Several years later Félix Kir returned triumphantly to Dijon, on the front of a French tank, as usual in a cassock. Shortly afterward, he was elected mayor of Dijon.

His would-be assassins were caught and put on trial right after the Liberation. The lawyer for the defendants, who were now in their late teens or early twenties, pleaded with Kir to forgive the young men, saying: "You are a man of the cloth, you should show Christian charity toward these young people. They didn't know what they were doing when they came to kill you."

Chanoine Kir exclaimed: "They knew exactly what they were up to, those Fascist bastards. C'étaient des salauds! Execute them!" and they were executed. Had the trial taken place two or three years later, they would probably have gotten off with a moderate jail sentence. But right after the Liberation, collaborators with the Nazis received no mercy.

For decades Félix Kir, who wanted to be called Monsieur le Maire and not Chanoine or Mon Père, was mayor of Dijon and an independent deputy from the department of the Côte d'Or in the National Assembly. He was just as conservative as General de Gaulle but Kir hated him for reasons he never made clear to me on my frequent visits to Dijon.

As mayor, Kir organized innumerable vins d'honneur in honor of visitors. Among his guests were people from 20 cities which he "twinned" with Dijon, among them Dallas. Of course, he served white wine and cassis cocktails. They soon became known as kirs. On one occasion, when I was visiting him, the mayor arranged a reception for 60 visitors from Skopje in Macedonia, a city he had twinned with Dijon after it had had a terrible earthquake.

As the two of us walked around the long table, Kir explained what should go into a proper kir: "Four parts of a good dry white wine from Burgundy, naturally, and one part cassis. You don't want it too sweet." (The traditional kir is two-thirds white wine and one-third cassis.) When he had filled 60 glasses, the Macedonians arrived.

He concluded his toast with the subversive words, "Vive la 6e République!" (Long Live the Sixth Republic!), showing what he thought of de Gaulle's fifth republic.

Like so many French people, Félix Kir was short on humor and long on wit. In a public debate with an atheist, the atheist asked him how he could possibly believe in God when he had never seen him. "Well," he retorted, "I've never seen my rear end either, but I know it's there."

Understandably, Monsieur le Maire was hugely popular in Dijon and the region and impossible to defeat in an election. When he died at the age of 92 in 1968, he was the oldest member of National Assembly.

Although conservative, Kir felt very strongly about the importance of peace. He twinned Dijon with Stalingrad. Nikita Khrushchev decided to call on the Chanoine in Dijon on a state visit to France. They were going to speak together from a balcony of the town hall to an enormous crowd. It was not to be. A car, apparently arranged by the Gaullist authorities in Paris, picked up or, rather, kidnapped the elderly mayor and drove him around the countryside for four or five hours until Khrushchev had come and gone.

On one visit I asked the mayor, who was in his late eighties, whether, for a picture, he would direct traffic at a major intersection. He got up at once on a podium, borrowed a white baton and a képi from a policeman and started directing traffic. Misdirecting traffic would be closer to the truth. He caused a terrific traffic jam which had everyone laughing. He really was a loose canon.

I wondered what Mayor Kir ate and drank on an average weekday. I found out when he invited me to lunch with him in a superb restaurant across from the city hall. "Let's have a kir to start with," he said. Then, he ordered two bottles of wine, one old Burgundy red for himself, and a sparkling Burgundy for me. He was under the impression that as an American, I would much prefer a sparkling Burgundy to any other kind. I wasn't able to decline the sparkling bottle or not to drink it. He finished his bottle and said, "Let's have something to finish off the lunch." He ordered a marc de Bourgogne.

"What are you going to do now?" I asked Kir at 3:30 in the afternoon. "Why, I'm going back to the city hall to work," he said, "and what about you?"

"I'm going back to the hotel to sleep it off," I replied.

Samovars to Tula

Philippe Lamour, in charge of development and management of the Lower Rhone and Languedoc region of southern France, was sharing an improvised podium in the countryside near Nimes with an illustrious visitor, Nikita Khrushchev, then head of the Soviet Union.

"This is France's California," Lamour declared enthusiastically, pointing in every direction. "We grow everything here and we'd like to increase our trade with you in the USSR."

"What do you propose to sell us?" Nikita asked.

"Potatoes," replied Lamour.

"You want to sell us Russians potatoes!" Khrushchev exclaimed in his own version of coals to Newcastle. "Why, there's an old Russian proverb, 'you don't take a samovar to Tula.'"

Tula, a city 100 miles south of Moscow, is still the center of samovar production. Except for samovar-seekers, the principal attraction nearby is the home and burial place of Tolstoy, where he wrote "War and Peace" and "Anna Karenina."

*　　*　　*

Harmonious Jingling Upon Words

The great American bald ego

In Latin America—preaching to the forcibly converted

Mass wisteria

Suffering from Scarlatti fever

Peter Ustinov on a Movie Lot

One obvious disadvantage of the Victorine Film Studio in Nice is its proximity to the airport, just across the seaside Promenade des Anglais. When you are directing a film about Italian anarchists in the 19th century, as Peter Ustinov was the day I turned up, the disadvantage is audible.

Half a dozen times the same scene had been shot, only to be ruined by the sound of a jet plane landing or taking off. The seventh time everything went perfectly, with no 20th century jet noise to be heard in 19th century Italy. Suddenly something like the sound of a landing jet, albeit decibels lower, could be heard belatedly. Expert at imitating racing cars, playful Peter was pretending to be a jet aircraft. He laughed uproariously even louder.

The next scene was to be in a bordello. "What do you think this bordello should look like?" the assistant director asked Ustinov.

"It ought to be the kind of a place you could take your family to on a Sunday morning," he suggested.

The two directors walked along a street in the lot that was lined with late 19th and early 20th century automobiles.

"Are you interested in old cars?" asked Peter.

"Oh, yes," replied the assistant film director. "I have an old, old Renault."

"What kind of fuel does it use?" Peter asked.

"It burns kerosene. Do you like old automobiles, too?"

"Yes, indeed," replied Peter. "I have an auto-da-fe. It burns heretics."

The Vanishing Vespasienne

Throughout their long history, the French have always urinated in the street. Furthermore, this propensity for public pissing has been untrammeled by any misplaced feeling of embarrassment.

In the Renaissance reign of François I, noblemen in wigs and lace customarily urinated on palace walls and on the statues of the kings of France.

In 1809 Napoleon's wife Josephine was accompanying him on his way to Spain. Passing through a Bordeaux vineyard, the empress suddenly felt an urgent need to pass water. Ever since then a Gironde wine bears the label with her effigy and the name "La Pissotière de l'Impératrice" (The Empress's urinal).

The tradition persisted and in 1934 the novelist Gabriel Chevallier set France a-laughing with "Clochemerle," a story about a village quarrel over the mayor's plan to put a new urinal near the church.

One of the best-known Corsican ethnic jokes concerns a chap in Marseilles who is peeing on a stationary trolley car when, unexpectedly, it pulls away leaving him face to face with a furious cop. "What the hell do you think you're doing? Let me see your identity papers. Ah, your name is Colombani, so you're a Corsican like me. Pisse, Colombani, pisse!"

Now, if the French didn't invent the pissoir, they popularized it. The honor of creating the first public urinal belongs to the first century Roman emperor, Titus Flavius Vespasianus. Not only did he place pissoirs in the streets of Rome but he leveled a tax on those who used them. It is unclear how he collected the tax.

In their heyday, 1930, there were no fewer than 1,230 "vespasiennes," as they came to be known, in the streets of Paris. Olive green, perforated metal rotundas with a glass roof and a luminous globe, they were as much a Paris landmark as the Eiffel Tower. In the 1930s not prosperity but a pissoir was just around the corner.

The first Parisian vespasienne appeared in 1833, thanks to the Prefect, Count Claude Phillibert de Rambuteau. From the outset these early vespasiennes, often perforated with the royalist fleur-de-lys, were expressions of male chauvinism for, as one writer put it, "They allowed the masculine part of the Paris population to find relief for the torture caused by intolerant bladders without disregarding elementary decency."

The protests were not long in coming. "Since women are the equals of men before nature," asserted an anonymous author in 1870, "why should they not be everyday equals in the streets of Paris?" An engineer named Jules Brunfaut urged urinals for women 10 years later, saying: "When will we think of doing for the weaker sex what has been done everywhere for the king of creation? When will our unfortunate companions be able to satisfy the most imperious demand of nature?"

After all, as Herodotus said (Tome II, page 287), "In Egypt women urinated standing up."

The first timid, but successful, attacks on vespasiennes were launched after World War II on the grounds that they froze up in winter and stunk to high heaven in summer. Besides, they were esthetically ugly.

In the 1940s and 1950s, they started disappearing. "Not so much because of the attacks on them," explained Joseph Calvet, a municipal engineer dealing with pissoirs, "but because they had ceased to be of public utility. For one thing, underground public lavatories sprang up everywhere. Anyway, these days who can't afford to enter a café, buy a cup of coffee and use the toilet? Many urinals had to be knocked down because they were in the way of widened streets, gas stations, parking lots, new housing. We got rid of those near schools and churches. They're fading away."

By 1954 there were only 567 pissoirs still standing, by 1966 a mere 329.

Not everyone applauded. City councilman René Fayssat took a dim view. "Doubtless they are unaesthetic," he told the city council, "but they occupied a good place in the paintings of the Impressionists. Modern painters haven't been afraid to make them part of the Paris landscape. Even if they're not pretty, we got used to them, didn't we?"

Fayssat went on to plead: "Don't abolish the pissoir. The absence of a vespasienne is of a nature to provoke or aggravate physical disorder among many people, notably elderly ones."

"I couldn't agree more," commented taxi driver Bernard Roton during a tour of the last remaining public urinals. "Funny thing how the last pissoirs are all in the working-class quarters of Paris. What makes the city authorities think that workers urinate more than bourgeois?"

In the summer of 2006, only one vespasienne out of the original 1,230 survived in the streets of Paris. It is located on Boulevard Arago on the Left Bank beneath the forbidding walls of Santé Prison. According to a city engineer, there are no plans to destroy this last of the Mohicans: "It's a monument of a Paris of another day."

Sic transit gloria vespasiannae. Another symbol of male chauvinism falls off the locomotive of history. If women never did win the right to use them, by wrinkling up their noses, they hastened their downfall.

Confusione Italiana

Before Roger Beardwood became Time Magazine's Paris bureau chief, he worked in London for the Financial Times. At a staff meeting the (then) editor of the FT, Sir Gordon Newton, told his reporters that he had encountered a nouveau riche at a vernissage on Venetian art the previous evening. "The fellow urged me to go to his house to view his latest acquisition for his art collection," explained Sir Gordon. "'What did you buy?' I inquired. 'A £100,000 Vaporetto,' said the collector."

"He knew nothing about art," Sir Gordon chortled to his staff. "He didn't mean a Vaporetto. Of course, he meant a Rigoletto."

In proposing a story on the FT to Time, Beardwood said, "Sir Gordon was just as ignorant about Venetian art as the nouveau riche. Obviously, he didn't mean Rigoletto, he meant a Cannelloni!"

*　　*　　*

Harmonious Jingling Upon Words

It's an old husband's tale

Methane, you Tarzan

As they say in Addis Ababa, it's haile unlikely, haile salacious

Bettleheim of the Republic

Her doctor is a general quacktitioner

He may mince meat but he doesn't mince words

On a Slippery Slope

It was the beginning of December and too early in the season to ski, so I looked around the Swiss resort for something to do. "Why don't you take a look at St Moritz's Olympic bobsled run?" the hotel concierge had suggested.

When a Swiss-German chap at the top of the Cresta Run saw me walking over in my suit and tie, overcoat and low city shoes, he grinned at his comrades and exchanged a few words in incomprehensible "schweitzerdeutsch," and said to me, "Care to take a ride down it?"

"Absolutely." I replied without hesitation.

"Four-man bob or two-man bob?"

"A two-man bob," I replied, not wishing to share the glory with three Swiss.

One of the chortlers clamped a helmet on my head, installed me on the bob behind the pilot, and gave our bobsled a good shove with his foot.

In less time than it takes to say Arnold Winkelried or even William Tell, I realized I had made a bad mistake.

At the very start my left hand was wrenched free and I held on desperately with the other hand. For a fleeting second I contemplated letting go with my right hand and sliding gently off the sled. But the speedy, twisting ride discouraged me. I abandoned the idea when we slammed off the icy walls, sometimes apparently flying upside down. Sky and ice were everywhere.

As the bobsled accelerated, the driver kept hollering at me. I thought this was a poor moment for conversation and just did my best to hold on. He went on shouting words into the wind. At long last, which is to say barely over a minute later, the sled slid to a stop at the finish line.

I jumped up, my legs buckled and I crumpled back onto the bobsled.

Green with fear and anger, the pilot leapt up and cried: "Are you mad? Didn't you hear me tell you to brake? You nearly killed us both!"

"Brake? I didn't know I was supposed to brake, and anyway you never told me where the brake was."

"We thought you knew. Nobody in his right mind goes down an Olympic bobsled run without braking."

Just then the loudspeaker announced that the team of Bumpernagel and Ress had broken the season's Olympic piste record in one minute and a few seconds.

I was elated; the pilot was not consoled.

Three years later in February I returned to St Moritz looking for a story. During a conversation with the resort's tourism director the subject turned to bobsleds.

"Wouldn't you like to go down our Olympic bobsled piste? It's really exciting. Anyway, you wouldn't be the first American journalist to do it. A few years ago an American reporter went down the run. He refused to brake and he set a course record that lasted throughout the whole season. What an incredibly courageous fellow he was!"

"Courageous?" I said, "He was a damned fool. It was me!"

*BRAKE!

A Writer and His Purring Pussies

"When you go to see André Malraux," advised an old friend of his, Pierre Viansson-Ponté, Le Monde's political editor, "don't pay any attention to his cats. Malraux loves cats and he's very possessive about them."

Good advice, but did I heed it?

I was taking notes on a spiral pad with a ballpoint pen when the first one made a purring entrance. I ignored him. Malraux grabbed him by the scruff of his neck and plunked him down on his knees. An unconscionable gesture for a cat-lover. As soon as he let go of the cat, the cat jumped off Malraux's lap to the floor. He looked around and I tried to pay no attention to him, but I love cats, too, so I winked. Promptly the cat hopped on to my lap.

"You won't be able to take notes with a cat on your lap," Malraux commented.

"I can manage," I replied, holding the pad and pen in mid-air.

The second cat joined the play. Malraux repeated his cat-in-the-lap gesture and eventually the cat jumped down, looked around and, with no encouragement from me, climbed up on my now crowded knees.

Disconcerted and possibly jealous, Malraux said, "You certainly won't be able to write with my two cats all over you!"

"Not really a problem," I insisted, poising pad and pen halfway to the ceiling.

The interview over, the novelist, Minister of Culture under de Gaulle, and the cleaner-up of the monuments of Paris remarked, "I think my cats prefer you to me."

"Not at all," I tried to reassure Malraux, "it's just that you unfortunately treated them like master-adoring dogs instead of free-thinking cats."

Back in the office, I called Time in New York to update the previous week's unpublished story on Malraux. Chatting with an editor, I realized I had no updater. So, I recounted the cat play, not intending that it be published. It was, to my embarrassment. I hastened to write an apology to André Malraux.

He replied at once with charming words: "I know only too well the constraints of the métier of journalism to hold the cat story against you."

A Breton Bulldozer

While researching a story in Brittany on the Breton language, I met Pierre Hélias, who was then broadcasting in Breton on Radio Quimper and later became a best-selling author.

"My name is obviously Greek in origin, but I'm a native Breton speaker," he told me.

"What characterizes the Breton language?" I inquired.

"It is remarkable for being able to express concrete ideas," he said, "but hopeless when it comes to expressing abstract concepts, philosophical thoughts."

"Give me an example," I urged Hélias.

"Eh bien, one day I was walking in the Breton countryside when I encountered a peasant on a bulldozer. I asked him in Breton, 'What do you call that machine in our language?'

"He replied, 'I call it a tourter.'

"'What's a tourter?' I asked.

"'A tourter,' he explained in French for me, 'is the Breton word for a calf sprouting horns. The horns itch and to calm the irritation, the calf rubs his head backwards and forwards on a tree trunk.' That reminded the peasant of the movement of his bulldozer. Q.E.D. the bulldozer was a tourter."

*　　*　　*

Harmonious Jingling Upon Words

Baroque artists had a gilt complex

When the volcano erupted, it was lava at first sight

Llama—a sheared natural resource

Keeping a low data profile

I'd obey the Popes' injunctions to practice coitus interruptus, if I were not afraid of having withdrawal symptoms

Dinners with Graham Greene

A dinner with Graham Greene in Antibes could start, so to speak, at lunch. As neither of us ever cooked, and there was only a small number of restaurants to be frequented in the Riviera resort, I often found myself lunching at the same restaurant as the writer. Almost invariably he would be reading a fat biography.

"May I sit down or would you prefer to go on reading?" I would ask respectfully.

"I should like to continue reading," he usually said, "but we could have dinner this evening."

Years earlier we had reached a modus vivaldi, whoops, vivendi, about our relationship. "We can be friends if you promise me not to take notes on what I say during a meal or afterwards. Then I shall be at ease with you. And no articles about me unless I agree to them." I willingly accepted these ground rules, and as neither of us had many friends in Antibes, we saw a lot of each other.

The dinner scenario hardly varied. It was always whisky, to start with. Only the brand changed. I'd drive to his city apartment overlooking the Antibes sea front. The streets were full of uncollected trash. "It's not the Côte d'Azur," he remarked once, "it's the côte d'ordure." It was the only pun I ever heard him make. He disliked puns, especially mine.

"Would you like a whisky?" he always began. "Will Grouse do?" Once he pointed to a bottle of whisky with a Japanese name, Santory, on it. It came with a letter, he explained. "They're offering me a free life-time supply of their whisky if I will have a character in one of my novels ask for that Japanese brand of scotch. What do you think I should do?"

I suggested mildly that he knew very well what to do. Anyway, I added, you've not tasted it yet. It was only several pre-dinner drinks later that the bottle was opened. It tasted pretty authentic to my uneducated palate. I didn't have the impression that he was overwhelmed. In any case, I was never offered a Japanese whisky again.

It was impossible to go out for dinner without two whiskies neat. Normally we debated where to go for dinner. But one night he said we'd go to a new place. "There's one problem with it, though," he admitted. "The chairs are dreadfully uncomfortable. Seventeenth century chairs, I suspect. They were given to the owner by his father-in-law and mother-in-law, so he can't get rid of them. We shall have to go there with pillows."

We always walked from Greene's centrally located flat to any of our half dozen restaurants. I felt a bit silly walking through the city carrying a largish pillow. He didn't. When we got to his new restaurant, horribile dictu, we found it closed. What to do with the pillows?

"Shouldn't we take them back to your apartment?" I suggested timidly.

"No," he said, "we'll just go across the street to the Venise" (one of his favorite restaurants).

It was summertime and of course there was no cloakroom attendant.

"Bonsoir, Monsieur Greene," said the owner, pleased to see his most famous customer.

Greene handed him his pillow and I did likewise. The restaurateur looked puzzled but said nothing.

"One of the reasons I like this place," Greene explained, "is that they don't object if I choose a pasta as the main course." He did just that, but compensated with a bottle of wine, which we shared.

We also shared the bill. Early on in the relationship, we took turns paying. But he didn't like this arrangement because he felt we never remembered whose turn it was. So, it was a Dutch treat.

As we were leaving, the restaurateur handed us the pillows, but could not resist inquiring, "Do you mind if I ask you why you came to my restaurant with pillows?"

Ha ha, I thought, now Graham will have to come up with an innovative explanation.

"We intended to eat in the restaurant across the street," said Greene bluntly, "but it was closed."

When we arrived in front of his apartment, Graham always proposed "a drink for the road." I never declined his invitation. I drove home extremely carefully. Even if I had wanted to make notes about our conversation, even if I had never promised to write about our encounters, I couldn't have recalled a tenth of what was said and what happened during the long alcoholic evenings.

Greene hated being recognized in a public setting. Every so often as he walked briskly through the streets of Antibes, a stranger would accost him and say, "Aren't you Graham Greene?"

"I glaze," he said, "or I reply, 'you must be thinking of my brother.' I stay away from television so that people won't recognize me. I agreed to appear on Budapest TV because I thought that was pretty safe.

"Actually there is another Graham Greene. I mean that's his name. We've never met but some day I'd like to do a story about us. Our paths keep crossing. The other Graham Greene was thrown into jail in Assam and wired the 'Picture Post' to send him a hundred pounds. The magazine contacted me and I offered to go to India and to write about our confrontation, but the plan didn't work out."

The writer visibly enjoyed chatting about his namesake. "One day I was in a hotel in Rome and a woman named Veronica called up. 'We met in Arabia,' she reminded me. Obviously she knew the other Greene because I had never been in Arabia. I suggested a drink in the bar. I didn't turn up, though, after a friend I sent ahead to the bar phoned me to say she was awful.

"On another occasion in London I bought a plane ticket to New York. The airline employee said, 'You're not staying very long in the States, are you? You're flying over on September 2 and returning the next day.' I told her I hadn't even thought of booking my return flight. Of course, the other G.G. was returning to London on September 3."

Contrary to what one might expect of an Englishman who had chosen to live in France, Greene much preferred English cooking to French cuisine. "Yes, French gigot [leg of lamb] is good," he conceded, "but British roast saddle of mutton is better. Our lamb cutlets are superior to the French. English sausages and beer are also much better. I'd choose English apple pie over French tarte aux pommes. And then I am very proud of Welsh rarebit, herring roes on toast and treacle tart."

Greene also had a weakness for Irish coffee. "I sleep comfortably after drinking one, but one night in a Paris restaurant the proprietor poured out Scotch whisky for want of Irish and the result was deplorable."

Advancing years didn't much alter Greene's fairly rigid work routine. Between breakfast (tea, dry biscuits and marmalade) at 8:30 and lunch at 12:15 he wrote "a minimum of 300 words a morning, if possible 400, six days a week. That's my quota. I can really write for an hour or an hour and a half at most. I like to stop in the middle of a scene because that makes it easier to start the next day. Writing a novel does not become easier with age and experience. Ever since I wrote 'A Burnt-Out Case' in 1959, I've thought that each novel was the last I'd be capable of writing." One day he complained that he was "down to only 250 words a morning. Deplorable."

When he wasn't writing—and he never did afternoons or evenings in Antibes—he was generally reading. Although he claimed to be a slow reader, he said he averaged 13 books a month. He liked Thomas Hardy's poetry, Browning and Evelyn Waugh. "I can read a Joseph Conrad novel three or four times, but pornography only once and then only in small doses. I find the present permissiveness rather boring. By the way, the French translation of my first published book, 'The Man Within,' was censored by Jacques Maritain on the grounds it was pornographic!"

That first novel sold 8,000 copies, an impressive number for 1929. "But I wasn't a commercially successful writer until after the war," he pointed out. "My first best seller, 'The Heart of the Matter,' was published in 1948. I was in debt to my publishers and wrote book reviews to make ends meet."

Greene thought so poorly of his second and third novels, which sold, respectively, only 2,000 and 1,200 copies, that he simply suppressed them from the list of his works. They have never been republished. "For a lot of money you could find them in a second-hand book shop. Their titles? Why should I help you?"

Did he think that "The Man Within" was satisfactory? "No," he admitted, "but you can't suppress them all. You have to have a first novel, don't you? Actually, 'The Man Within' was the third book I had written, but the first two were turned down by publishers. If 'The Man Within' had not been published, I would have stopped writing."

Greene objected to being called "a Catholic writer. I don't believe I have even gone so far as to describe myself as a novelist who writes about Catholic themes. I am a writer who happens to be a Catholic. No one knew I was a Catholic until 'Brighton Rock' and I had been writing then for 10 years."

Another legend about Graham Greene had him entering and winning all the literary contests of the New Statesman wherein readers were invited to write "in the style of Graham Greene."

"I've entered quite a few competitions of this sort," he acknowledged, "but I have rarely won. Once I did win a second prize for the first paragraph of a Greene novel, under an assumed name, naturally. I wrote a plot on another slip of paper and Mario Soldati made a film out of it in Venice with Trevor Howard. It was called 'The Stranger's Hand' and my hand appeared on a gondola."

Greene strongly disliked just about every film version of his novels or "entertainments," the exception being "The Third Man," which most people didn't realize he had written. What Greene liked best was "when a director, like Otto Preminger, acquired an option, for example, for 'A Burnt-Out Case,' let it lapse once, re-acquired it, allowed the option to lapse a second time, and then never made the movie."

Greene admitted that "the money was a temptation, but the cinema versions of my novels always turned out so awful."

Four or five of Greene's novels were situated in Latin America and the Caribbean, and he was keenly interested in the region's politics. The overthrow and murder of Salvador Allende, whom Greene knew and admired, and the persecution of his supporters filled him, as he put it to me, "with grief and horror."

"If I had to classify myself politically, I suppose I would say I was a humanist and a socialist. Rather like Dubcek. I am certainly on the left. The destruction of the courageous Chilean effort to build socialism with a human face leaves one terribly, terribly sad. It was the way I felt when I learned of Che Guevara's death."

Greene used to feel that "The Power and the Glory," one of his early books, was his best novel. "I no longer think that," he said. "Now I believe that 'The Honorary Consul' is my best book of fiction."

But didn't all creative artists think that their most recent work was their finest, I suggested? Didn't Charlie Chaplin unhesitatingly describe "Limelight," as soon as he had shot it, as the best film he had ever made?

"I have seldom thought that the last thing I did was the best," he replied. "This time, with 'The Honorary Consul,' I do. It has certainly given me more trouble than previous novels. There were moments when I realized perfectly why Hemingway shot himself one day. I was nearly halfway through it before I was sure I'd finish it. I wrote the novel seven times, eight times in fact, since in addition to the seven typescripts there was the original manuscript. I always write books longhand. My two fingers on the typewriter don't connect with my brain. My hand on a pen does. A fountain pen, of course. Ballpoint pens are good only for filling in forms on planes."

Long before publication of the book-that-was-almost-not-written, the Book-of-the-Month Club selected it. It was Greene's third Book Club choice, after "A Burnt-Out Case" and "Travels with My Aunt." Le Monde, France's most prestigious newspaper, and a German daily asked Greene for permission to serialize the novel in toto.

"I refused," said Greene, "because the rhythm of a novel is destroyed by daily excerpts."

Well, if Greene was not always convinced that his most recent book was his best, was he, like so many artists, bored with the work he had just finished?

"Oh, I'm not bored with it," he exclaimed unconvincingly, "but with life."

A Test of Food Prejudices

There was a bistro in the old town of Nice that tested a man's and a woman's fortitude in regard to food. La Trappa specialized in innards, such as brain, tripe, kidneys, and sheep's testicles. Mind you, the sheep's testicles were breaded.

When visitors arrived on the Riviera, I liked to take them to La Trappa to test their gourmet pretensions. One such visitor was the Italian film director, Michelangelo Antonioni. His companion, the very attractive Italian actress, Monica Vitti, didn't share his pretensions.

"Does Nice have a specific cuisine that isn't French or Italian?" Antonioni asked.

"Yes," I said, "there's a restaurant called La Trappa that is Niçois."

"What are their specialties?" the Italian gourmet inquired, when the three of us were seated.

"Innards."

Antonioni grimaced.

"Perhaps you just want a steak with French fries," I suggested.

"No, no, no," said Antonioni, "what else could I have?"

"Well, for example, tripe or breaded sheep's testicles."

Monica decided for us: "You have the tripe, Michele, I'll have a coq au vin, and our journalist friend will take the sheep's testicles."

It all arrived. Antonioni tasted the tripe, one might say gingerly, and pronounced it "the best tripe I have ever had." Monica was less enthralled with the muddy-looking coq au vin. She looked at what I was eating, one might say with relish, and asked if she might taste it. "Of course," I agreed.

Smacking her lips with delectation, Monica pushed the plate of breaded sheep's testicles at Antonioni, and said, "Taste them, Michele, they may do you some good."

Another visitor was Terry Spencer, a Life magazine photographer. He spent an entire morning on the beach at Nice shooting pictures of Jacques Cousteau's floating laboratory 30 or 40 yards offshore. It wasn't exhausting, but it was boring.

Finally, at midday, Terry inquired, "Have you any ideas where we might have a good lunch?"

"Yes," I replied, "if you don't have any food prejudices."

"No, I don't have any. I'm British not American." I didn't argue with him.

"La Trappa in the old town has great food, but it's mostly innards. Does that turn you off?"

Terry had been in the RAF during World War II, was shot down, escaped from a POW camp, made his way to England, was put back in the RAF, shot down a second time, and freed from a POW camp by the Russians.

"So, you think I'm afraid of innards?"

At La Trappa he ordered the sheep's testicles, flat, light-colored patties, and loved them. "Tomorrow my wife Lesley will join us and we'll play a trick on her. She really only likes steak, nothing exotic."

Another morning of photographing Cousteau's floating lab left Lesley Spencer as bored as I had been the day before. "At least we deserve a fine lunch," she said.

"We'll have that," said Terry. "Yesterday Paul took me to a great restaurant."

We made sure that Lesley didn't see the menu, as she would have immediately recognized the word that was almost the same in English as in French. Terry told her what there was to eat. She chose a coq au vin, and naturally he had the testicles described to the waitress in her own slang as "couilles."

While Terry was enjoying his dish, Lesley was unhappily fiddling with the coq au vin. "Could we exchange dishes?" she asked. Pretending reluctance, Terry said, "All right if you really want to." Lesley obviously liked the breaded testicles very much, until, that is, Terry asked her triumphantly, "Guess what you're eating."

Lesley put down her fork and knife at once. "We are not playing games," she said. "Tell me immediately what I have been eating."

"Oh, come on," said Terry, "give a guess." She said brain. "Much worse than that," he exclaimed.

"I insist on knowing what you had me eat," Lesley said angrily.

"Testicles!" Terry shouted.

"Whose?" cried Lesley.

The Duke of Windsor

An Associated Press photo of the Duke of Windsor watching Jack Nicklaus and Arnie Palmer play golf on a course near Paris caught the eye of Sports Illustrated in New York.

"Please interview the Duke on how he feels about golf and other sports. You can offer him up to $1,500 for a 1,500-word story that you would write," ran the S.I. telex.

I walked from the St. Nom-la-Bretèche clubhouse across several fairways looking for the Duke. That gave me time to consider just how I would address the former King of England and how I would go about offering him money. I had little experience in doing either.

"Your Royal Highness," I began cautiously, "Sports Illustrated has asked me . . ."

"Shhhush," he interrupted, from his seat on a shooting stick. "Mr. Palmer is about to hit the ball."

We walked for several more holes and I managed only to propose a story about sports based on a chat with him. He didn't seem interested, but I persisted.

"Your Majesty, naturally you are a very busy man and we couldn't expect you to work on a story for Sports Illustrated without some kind of compensation, I mean, we would want to uh, err," I mumbled on.

Abandoning the idea of bargaining by starting at perhaps $1,000, I added, "What would you say, Your Highness, to, err, $1,500?"

The Duke replied at once: "Now you're talking!" But, he added: "I shall have to take this up with the Duchess. And I would like a letter from Henry Luce, confirming this. He is a very close friend."

"It might be difficult to contact Mr. Luce [the founder of Time Magazine and Sports Illustrated] over the week-end," I said. "Would a letter from the Time Magazine Paris bureau chief, Curtis Prendergast, be acceptable?" Yes, it would.

Trotting back to the clubhouse and my car, I was astonished to bump into the Chairman of the Board of Time Inc., Jim Linen, who was an organizer of the Canada Cup Golf Tournament. I explained the problem.

"Lead me to your Duke," said Linen.

A few holes along they met. "This is Mr. Linen, Chairman of the Board of Time Inc.," I said to the Duke. "Mr Linen, the Duke of Windsor."

"Mr. Ress is a bona fide correspondent of Sports Illustrated and we'd like you to help him write a story about your views on sports," Mr. Linen said reassuringly. Then, reaching for his wallet, he pulled out a business card and wrote on it: "We owe you $1,500."

"Thank you," said the Duke, "I shall put this card in my wallet so I shan't lose it. You will send the check to my Swiss bank account?"

The next afternoon I turned up at the Bois de Boulogne residence of the Duke and Duchess, put at their disposal by the City of Paris at a small symbolic rent. Charles and Yvonne de Gaulle lived in it before them.

"Did you ever make a hole-in-one?" I asked. "Yes, three of them," he replied.

And had he played anyone famous? "When I was young, I played Emperor Hirohito. I beat him badly, but perhaps you shouldn't write that. It might hurt his feelings. I also played against Bing Crosby and Tom Dewey. No, course, I didn't beat Bing. He was much too good for me."

What other sports did he like? "I love American football, but perhaps we shouldn't write that either because the British might feel that I was discriminating against rugger [rugby]."

The next day, Sunday, I returned with a text of 1,300 words. There was no way of squeezing 1,500 words out of the conversation with the Duke, whom I was now addressing as "Sir." I learned later that the proper form of address was "Your Grace."

While he was editing my story, tush-tushing, and crossing out line after line, anecdote after anecdote, the Duke explained: "I always use red ink. That way people know they're my corrections."

By this time the text was down to just under 1,100 words. Nevertheless, the Duke and eventually Sports Illustrated seemed pleased with it.

"I hope," I wired the magazine, "you like the way I write the ex-king's English."

4, ROUTE DU CHAMP D'ENTRAINEMENT

BOIS DE BOULOGNE . PARIS, 16°

SABLONS 86-51 . WINFIELD

November 14th, 1963

Dear Mr. Ress,

Thank you for your letter of
November 5 and for sending me a copy of "Sports
Illustrated" containing my article in connection
with the Canada Cup at St-Nom-la-Bretèche.

I take this opportunity of reaffirm-
ing my appreciation of your assistance in the
preparation of this short piece and my pleasure
in working with you. The Duchess who is my
severest critic, liked the article too.

I also enjoyed reading Henry
Longhurst's reportage of the tournament. He
writes well and with humor. It was too bad that
fog caused that last day's anticlimax.

Sincerely yours,

Edward

Duke of Windsor

Mr. Paul Evan Ress
Time-Life
17 Avenue Matignon
Paris 8°

Miró, Miró on the Wall

I was standing in Joan Miró's atelier in his home in Palma de Majorca, staring at little red and blue figures or abstract objects filling a canvas. A voice behind me said, "I know what you're thinking." The voice belonged to Aimé Maeght, the famous Catalan painter's well-known art dealer.

"No, you don't," I retorted. "What do you think I was thinking?"

"That you could paint that picture as well as Miró did."

"No, I don't imagine any such thing, but I do believe that either of my daughters could do a better painting."

Maeght admitted that Miró looks very easy to imitate. "Once I commissioned a highly skilled Louvre restorer of 18th century Dutch landscapes to do a fake Miró for me," he explained. "Well, after three or four months he came to see me and confessed he had failed. 'It's impossible to do a false Miró. He can't be imitated,' he said."

Maeght went on to say that "there are many more imitation Picassos, Braques and Matisses than there are fake Mirós floating around in the art world and turning up at auctions."

I took Maeght's word for it for who was I to contest the opinion of one of the world's leading art dealers?

To Bee or Not To Bee

In the "old days" when Slovenia was a Yugoslav republic, souvenir-hunting tourists would enter a shop in downtown Ljubljana and ask to see some ikons.

"We don't have ikons. Slovenians are Roman Catholics, not Greek or Russian Orthodox Catholics," saleswomen explained. "Wouldn't you like a beehive painting instead?"

"What kind of a painting did you say?" the perplexed tourist usually asked.

He or she was then shown a pile of beehive panels, each measuring just under 12 inches long and not quite 5 inches wide. Some were religious in character; others were secular, often strong on social satire.

When I first made a beeline for Slovenia in 1966, a painted panel reproduction of an old, original 18th or 19th century beehive panel sold for around 4,000 dinars or slightly over $3. Today, 40 years later, a hand-painted panel goes for 4,000 to 5,000 tollars, i.e., $20 to $25.

No originals are to be found. They have all been bought up by antique-shop owners, interior decorators, museums and private collectors. Many of these collectors used to scour the countryside looking to buy authentic 19th century panels, rather like American antique lovers going to auctions and old farmhouses in search of butter bowls and rocking chairs. Since authentic old beehive paintings are extremely rare, when the president or premier of a country visits Slovenia, the custom is to give him or her a superb reproduction of a 19th century painted panel.

The oldest beehive panel is dated 1758 and can be seen in a museum entirely devoted to beekeeping and beehive art, the Museum of Apiculture, in the town of Radovljica in northwestern Slovenia. This panel shows Mary as a pilgrim with baby Jesus.

The Radovljica museum's curator, Ida Gnilsak, has preserved one of the country's finest collections of painted beehive panels and exhibited them beautifully. In all, there are about 400 originals. They trace the roughly 150-year history of beehive art from the middle of the 1700s to its decadence in the early 1900s.

In the beginning, most of the panels that decorated the beehives of Slovenian Alpine beekeepers had religious motifs. Favorite themes showed the Virgin Mary, Jesus chasing the money-changers from the temple, Saint Florian, the patron saint of beekeepers who protected them from fire, the Prodigal Son, Job, and the Three Wise Men. If crucifixions were rare, nativity scenes were common. The deep Catholicism of beekeepers is visible in one well-known and frequent panel showing devils driving Martin Luther and his wife in a carriage to Hell. To be sure that viewers would get the point, the name of Martin Luther appears in big letters on the stagecoach door.

In the 1830s and 1840s a large number of beehive panels depicted Old Testament stories such as Noah and the Ark, Adam and Eve, Joshua and the battle of Jericho, and Solomon's Judgments. One estimate puts the proportion of Old Testament panels at 21% and New Testament panels at 27%. This is rather surprising because there are relatively few Old Testament scenes in European folk art.

Early in the 1800s beehive panels with non-religious themes appeared. There were battle scenes of Serbian warriors vanquishing turbaned Turks (who occupied what became Yugoslavia for five centuries) and Slovenian peasants asking mercy from Napoleon's soldiers. From time to time religious themes reappeared. One such painting showed a peasant praying in front of a church at midday while appreciative angels led the oxen and plowed in his place. The moral of the story was clear to any Slovenian mountaineer: praying was not a waste of time and would be rewarded.

The good and bad sides of Slovene mountaineers, the lives they led, the views they held were all depicted with humor, often at their own expense, on secular beehive panels. For example, beekeepers thought poorly of tailors. Reflecting the dreadfully slow pace of tailors' work, panels had a tailor with a snail on a leash, or a tailor with sheers and pressing irons unable to catch up with a snail.

The Alpine Slovenians thought no better of hunters. They must be lazy or why would they have so much time to hunt? Perhaps the most famous beehive painting is that of a hunter's funeral. Happy hares carry a stretcher with the dead hunter on it, preceded and followed by four cheerful-looking foxes shouldering muskets topped by hats, and led by psalm-chanting bears. Beneath the stretcher walk the hunter's two dejected dogs. This beehive painting could serve as an emblem of the Society for the Prevention of Cruelty to Animals.

Scenes of village life were popular. There were panels of plowing, sowing, harvesting, grass-cutting and filling a hayrick; of builders, butchers, shoemakers, blacksmiths, seamstresses, charcoal-makers, barrel-makers and, of course, beekeepers all at work. Other paintings had a wife catching her husband being unfaithful. Napoleon wasn't popular in the Slovenian Alps, so when a French soldier, sitting in a cradle and most probably drunk, ordered a farmer to rock him, he was rocked so hard that in an adjoining panel he fell out of the cradle.

Other favorite targets of beehive artists were tax collectors, gendarmes and brigands.

So-called medieval "world-upside-down" panels show animals in human roles, such as rabbits roasting a hunter on a spit and animals judging and sentencing hunters.

Some panels are factual, others imaginary. Still others portray fairy tales or allegories. All told, somewhat more than half have non-religious subjects, and fully 97% of them are figurative. Landscapes are rare.

It will come as a surprise to no one that in the 1800s, in the Slovenian Alps, male chauvinism flourished. One beehive panel had a devil sharpening a woman's tongue on a grindstone, while another (a man's dream and a woman's wish) has an ugly old woman pass through a mill to emerge young and beautiful. Still another panel, probably with an original theme, shows a woman linen-maker lusting after a man "even if it's the devil himself," she says, which is precisely whom she gets. In a much reproduced panel, called "The Battle for a Man's Trousers," a fellow holds a pair of pants on a fishing line while three women in a stream try to get a bite on it.

Then there's the scene of two farmers pulling at the opposite ends of a cow they both covet, while a lawyer, dressed as a city dweller, tries to milk her.

In the mid-1800s American Indians in feathered headdresses suddenly made a mysterious appearance on beehive panels. One of them showed Indians threatening a captured white woman with a tomahawk. The explanation for this apparent mystery was simple. A Slovenian priest, Friderik Baraga, went to Michigan and the Great Lakes region to do missionary work. He came home and in 1837 wrote a book entitled "A Description of the Customs and Behaviour of the Indians of North America," in which there is a prominent story about Indians kidnapping two white girls. Beehive painters wasted no time illustrating Baraga's book.

What gave Slovenian beekeepers the idea of decorating their apiaries? One explanation was that beekeepers were very religious and panels showing Jesus, Mary, saints, and crosses could be considered "apotropaic," that is, a safeguard against evil. The panels would protect the bees from harm, such as disease parasites and bad weather. Like branding cattle, painting beehives made it easier for beekeepers to identify their hives and bees. After all, the beehouses stood right next to each other in the meadow. Some serious souls even suggested that the painted panels helped the bees to "find their way home."

All right, but why did beehive art develop only in three regions of Slovenia (all of Carniola, southern Carinthia and northwestern Styria), which now form a large part of the new, independent republic, instead of among religious beekeepers in other Alpine countries? When I asked the art historian Dr. Emilijan Cevc (pronounced say-oos) for his explanation, he replied with a quip, "Why does a meteor land where it does on earth?" But he conceded that there are good answers to this obvious question.

Like others who have looked into beehives (wearing masks), Cevc felt that the birth of beehive art owed a great deal to the flourishing state of folk art in Slovenia, particularly rich in the 1800s. "Slovenian artists," he said, "had a fertile imagination, a strong pictural sense, and a developed Baroque imagery. Beehive art is the legitimate child of Baroque art. It would be a mistake to consider beehive painting a rustic art."

According to another serious Slovenian student of beehive art, Boris Orel, who was director of the Slovene Ethnographic Museum after World War II, "The form of the Slovenian beehive partly accounted for its development in the 1700s when beekeeping and folk art flourished side by side in Slovenia." Besides, the region has been for centuries a center of well-developed and innovative beekeeping.

The first beehive was a long, squarish tube shaped rather like a tree trunk. Indeed, it no doubt evolved out of natural tree trunks. Later it came to resemble a five-year-old child's conventional drawing of a house. The 18th century Slovenian beehive offered a small flat surface "and this surface or panel provided people's painters [i.e., folk artists] with a new place for giving vent to their artistic and decorative urge," Orel continued.

The other places were intimidating church altars and walls (frescoes) and peasant dwellings (wood carving). The modest dimensions of the beehive panels also encouraged folk artists to paint on them. "They would never have dared to paint large canvases," Orel said. There was quite a market for good artists because the façade of a beehouse containing several hives could hold as many as 50 or 60 panels. The richer the ensemble of beehive art, the wealthier the owner passed for being. In modern lingo, beehive paintings became a status symbol.

It should be noted that panels were neither nailed nor glued to the hive. Like stones chipped to fit closely together without mortar, the panels were trimmed and whittled until they could be inserted snugly into the façade.

The colors were strong and vivid with reds and blues, yellows and ochres dominating. Judging the true colors of a beehive painting inside a dark museum room is like trying to determine the exact shade of the cloth in a tailor's back room. After all, the panels were painted for an open-air gallery.

No two panels of the same color were ever placed next to each other, so they were suited for close viewing. But from a distance they gave the overall impression of a mosaic. This was not coincidental, painters were quite aware of it.

Considering their exposure to wind and rain, humidity and sun (most beehives faced south), beehive paintings have survived remarkably well. The principal reason for this is undoubtedly the artists' technique of mixing their own colors out of home-made earth paints mixed with linseed oil. They used plants and herbs, pine and fir wood. Like the purple dye of the Phoenicians or the acoustics of Greek stadiums, the composition of Slovenian beehive painters' colors is a mystery today.

Beehive painters were more interested in line than in color and they drew well. When the elements did get the best of the paint, they left fine wood etchings. But weather was not the only enemy of beehive artists. The bees themselves bumbled things up occasionally by doing mass calisthenics near the hive aperture.

"These inexplicable gymnastics wore away the paint on the façade panels," said Cevc waspishly. Although it behooved the bees to behave at the beehive, sometimes they didn't.

The painting process itself was quite simple. First, a smoothed softwood board was covered with a light-colored oil paint. When it was completely dry, artists sketched, usually freehand. Sometimes, though, they used patterns or stencils. They would execute a drawing on paper, go over the outline with paint and then press the paper onto the wood. The impression created formed the basis for the picture. Another method was to use paper stencils on which a drawing was outlined with small holes. They laid the paper on the panel and went over it with a cloth bag containing ground pigment, thus creating an outline of the desired image in small dots.

How many beehive panels were painted and how many have survived? No one knows with certainty how many were painted, but Dr. Gorazd Makarovic, former curator of the Slovene Ethnographic Museum in Ljubljana and co-author with the current curator, Bojana Rogelj Skafar, of "Painted Beehive Panels," probably the best book on the subject, offers "as a rough guideline figure, at least 50,000 painted beehive panels." If anything, that would seem to be a modest estimate since a census of hives in the Carniola region alone in 1890 showed that there were close to 50,000 hives. Although not every hive had painted panels, those that did could easily have four or five dozen panels.

The museum in Ljubljana has an even larger collection of old and authentic panels than the Apiculture Museum in Radovljica—752, to be exact. Makarovic, the leading expert in the field, and Rogelj Skafar say that there are 3,000 panels preserved in museums and private collections. What complicates the count is the huge number of post-World War II reproductions. Some of these are very good indeed, others are mediocre and couldn't possibly be confused with a genuine 19th century beehive painting. Makarovic reckons there are around 600 themes or motifs among the 3,000 preserved panels.

The golden age of beehive panels was a period of about 40 or 50 years between 1830 and 1880, although well-known Slovene artists painted fine panels in the second half of the 18th century and early decades of the 19th century. One of the first was Slovenia's most famous beekeeper, Anton Jansa, who lived from 1734 to 1773 and lectured on apiculture at the court of Empress Maria

Theresa in Vienna. Another excellent beehive artist was Leopold Layer, one of Slovenia's finest classical painters, who lived, as the French say, on horseback over the 18th and 19th centuries. Layer was criticized for dabbling in beehive art but as he lacked commissions and money, he was not too proud to adorn hives.

Nor were the 19th century landscapist, Marko Pernhart, and Stefan Subic, a church fresco master. "They navigated financial straits directly to beehives," said Orel. Incidentally, Pernhart did not do landscapes on hive panels because beekeepers were not interested in landscapes and saw no point to them. Children are almost never depicted on beehive panels either because they had little social value in rural life.

Beehive paintings demonstrated wealth. This became very important in the rural environment, especially after the agro-industrial revolution of 1750-1835, which created an escalating social division based on wealth. In such a society there is usually a need to show off one's superior social position, greater prestige and riches. This need is an expression of personal and family vanity, as well as an aspiration toward social stability. In the Slovene rural society of this period it was more important to have than to be. Decorating the most valuable possessions, such as furniture and buildings, represented a way of emphasizing their material value. Apiaries were one of the most valuable possessions. In a late 17th century register of farm holdings in Carinthia, a beehive was worth twice as much as a pig or a sheep. Beekeepers were the very prosperous upper class of Slovene rural communities.

The culture of painting was shaped primarily during Sunday church-going. In the minds of the mostly illiterate rural population in the 1700s and 1800s, painting had great significance. Country folk felt that painted objects should not only have an esthetic role, being beautiful and interesting, but other utilitarian functions. Beehive panels were useful in many ways—warding off thieves and harm, and helping beekeepers and bees to find their hives.

Most apiaries sat in meadows and fields, but some stood in towns and villages. So, beehive panels were constantly on display. Even those who were not particularly interested were still familiar with them. Like church frescoes, the religious panels were meant to educate and influence the largely illiterate Slovene mountaineers. The secular panels, which mocked tailors and hunters, city folk and women, and many others, were designed to entertain and amuse passers-by.

The most prolific beehive artist of the 19th century and perhaps of the 150-year span of the art was Marija Pavlic, a disabled woman, who was taught by her father, also a rural painter. She derived her entire income from beehive panels. Her life from 1821 to 1891 covered the peak period of beehive art. Her earliest panel was dated 1838 when she was only 17 years old; the last panel was done in 1891, the year of her death.

"Although we recognize the style of 42 different beehive panel painters," says curator Bojana Rogelj Skafar, "we don't know the names of the majority of them. Marija Pavlic is perhaps the exception because her style is so familiar. Her panels are recognizable from their overall appearance, clear blocks of color and the very distinctive type of face used in all her characters."

Given the mid-18th century origin of beehive art, it is surprising that the first independent article on beehive art was written so much later in 1840. Michael Heinko not only provides a description of a Carniolan apiary, including its panels, but offers a witty commentary on some characteristic panel motifs.

Bojana Rogelj Skafar quotes Heinko: "Each hive is decorated with a picture which, experience indubitably shows, marks the homes of the little winged aeronauts so that they do not in error find themselves in a neighboring nest—the same function that house numbers perform for mankind, but not completely successfully as, regrettably, instances do occur of weak-sighted members of this species who do not see the house number and, in error, enter a strange house and even, absentmindedly, carry off articles not belonging to them. Perhaps it would be better if houses, instead of being numbered, followed the model of the Carniolan beehive, and were decorated with pictures."

Heinko's 1840 article also includes a sharp, amusing attack on one frequently repeated panel painting, that of the devil sharpening a woman's tongue upon a whetstone: "I am prepared to revive the sect of iconoclasts from the 8th century and to lead them against the beehives to do away with these scandalous and insulting lampoons of ladies. I am totally convinced that I would have nothing to fear, for the female leadership of the bee community would be inclined to support this action."

Michael Heinko was obviously way ahead of his time.

It is also surprising that from Heinko's pioneering text in 1840 until the early years of the 20th century, absolutely nothing more was written about beehive art. And yet this was a period when these panels were in great demand and production of them was at its peak.

In these five or six decades museum curators were not interested at all in the living folk art of beehive painting. They preferred to collect Celtic and Roman antiquities.

Then in 1905 Walter Schmidt, an archeologist, a beekeeper, and a collector for the Carniolian Land Museum, was one of the first to speak highly of beehive art. "With the panels," he said, "ordinary people could depict their lives, using religious, philosophical and, above all, humorous images."

It was about this time—the early 1900s—that the Slovene urban middle class became aware of beehive art. They started to consider it a "national heritage" and to refer to "our beehive panels."

But it was also the period in which beehive painting suffered an eclipse. By the end of World War I it had virtually disappeared. For once beehive painting experts—ethnographers, museum directors, academicians and academics, beekeepers—agreed on the causes of the demise of beehive art. Spacious Carniolan-type hives gave way to "A to Z" beehives that provided little or no space for the panels. Grazing conditions deteriorated as cattle chased bees from the meadows and fields. Sugar, which was cheaper to produce than honey, replaced it. Electricity sharply reduced the demand for wax candles. Meanwhile, beehive painting, now dependent on lower-quality industrialized paints, also declined and virtually disappeared. Bees became unemployed or at least under-employed.

World War I was a watershed in rural culture between agrarian values and those of an industrialized society in its relations to the world and also to the paintings of beehive panels as a craft. In the years leading up to the war, professional and semi-professional artists had pretty much stopped painting panels and rural beekeepers produced their own (less talented) reproductions of traditional panels.

In 1929 Stanko Vurnik, custodian of the Royal Ethnographic Museum, was the first savant to address the subject of beehive panels in detail. He called them "a unique feature of Slovene folk art which no other nation possesses." The paintings interested him "as a visual source of representations of the rural Slovene imagination, its lively vision and healthy, robust, humorous substance, artistically dressed in extremely decorative sensual form."

In his 1951 essay, Boris Orel pointed to the economic importance of apiculture in the 1700s and 1800s and the flowering of decorative folk art in those centuries. "There came about," he wrote, "a fortuitous and successful union between the most up-to-date beekeeping practices, with its particular form of beehive, and folk painting which was at its artistic peak. Beehive art in the Slovene Alps is unique in the world."

While that describes the material conditions which made beehive painting possible and thrive for a century and a half, it still doesn't entirely explain why the art suddenly emerged in the Slovene Alps. As one beehive art expert put it, "It is inexplicable. It is a product of the marvelous world of the human creative spirit."

Why did it catch on only in the Slovene Alps? The favorable form of the beehives, the wealth of the beekeepers, the rich traditions of Baroque painting, the sense of humor of the rural population and their willingness to make fun of themselves—all these existed in the Slovene Alps but nowhere else all together.

In 1967 the first major beehive art exhibition took place in Ljubljana at the Slovene Ethnographic Museum. Instead of being a subject of interest to a handful of experts and to beekeepers, the painted panels now turned into a collectors' passion for thousands of ordinary city dwellers. They spent weekends combing the mountainous countryside to find and buy old beehive panels. Like philatelists, panel-collectors swapped beehive paintings. It wasn't long before beehive panels became a rarity precisely when the demand for them grew enormously.

With original beehive paintings next to impossible to find, expensive when available, and the demand vastly exceeding the supply, there was only one solution: produce by hand large numbers of inexpensive copies of old panels. A small fortune awaited the painter who understood this. One who did was Vid Sedej (pronounced sed-day) whose father was a renowned Slovene academic painter. He had schooled Vid in Slovene folk art since childhood.

"While other artists seek their inspiration in modernism," says Vid, "I have always been attracted by animal pictures and subjects of folk art. The subject matter comes from an inner inspiration. My paintings reflect my thinking about the world." Sedej once received an order from a Catholic religious community which still possesses several monasteries and convents in Slovenia where they kept bees. "I was never sure whether the panels were meant to adorn their hives or their cells."

One day in 1966, Vid Sedej said to me sadly, "I fear I am the last of the beehive painters."

Not so! There has been a lively revival of beehive art. Quite a few artists have followed in Sedej's footsteps. There is a substantial market for them in individual collectors who decorate the furniture and walls of their home with modern panel reproductions of old traditional themes. Then there are regular exhibitions of beehive art. Beekeeping is also enjoying a renaissance. Beekeepers with new hives look for panels. And finally tourist shops sell them in large quantities as souvenirs to tourists. The beehive panels are picturesque, often very funny and small in size, easy to pack in a suitcase or a backpack. Now that Slovenia, a country of 2 million people half the size of Switzerland, has joined the European Union, many more foreign visitors—potential purchasers of panels—are expected.

Milan Plesec, 54, is typical of the new generation of beehive panel painters. "I have been collecting original ones for 40 years," he says. "It's a passion. People hear about me from friends, by word of mouth, and they visit my atelier. Some want me to repair or restore their panels. Others want new panels with the old themes. For a big exhibition in London in 1983-84, I was commissioned to create 300 panels. I use modern colors but in the old way with linseed oil." Plesec paints around 200 panels a month.

When Janko Zupanc retired to the Sava River port of Lancovo, he decided to become a beekeeper. First, he read all about bees and beekeeping. Then he built a bee-house, an apiary, and filled it with 300,000 young and old bees in six hives. Naturally he wished to decorate the façade with traditional painted panels. So, he looked around for a panel painter and found a woman artist in a nearby village. She filled the bill.

Commenting on the revival of beehive art, Bojana Rogelj Skafar, curator of the country's Ethnographic Museum, said, "Slovenes love bees. Maybe they see in bees something of their own stereotyped character, because, like themselves, bees are hard-working, productive, and not talkative."

An Angry Architect

Shortly before the great architect Le Corbusier finished the construction of a church in Ronchamp in the Vosges mountains of eastern France, I turned up to do a story about it. Since Le Corbusier (born Charles-Edouard Jeanneret) had a reputation of being very difficult to approach and of disliking American journalists particularly, I took the precaution of contacting a member of the leftwing Catholic city council that had commissioned the church and asking him to accompany me to the construction site. I had no thought of bumping into Le Corbusier, but just in case.

As we got close to the boat-shaped church, we were stopped by Le Corbusier himself.

"Who gave you permission to look at my church?" he said to me, glaring.

"This gentleman whom you will recognize as a member of the Ronchamp city council," I replied.

I quickly decided I had better ask him an intelligent question, not for example something silly that would irritate him, such as "How much did it cost to build this church?"

"Maître," I began cautiously, "does one have to have faith to build a church today?"

I asked the question knowing that Le Corbusier was a Protestant, an agnostic if not an atheist, and a descendant of the medieval Albigensian heretics.

Le Corbusier's reaction was furious. "You American journalists," he said, "are all impertinent." He turned his back on us and stalked off. I saw him once again sunning himself on a Riviera beach but made a point of not approaching him.

"Why," I asked the city councilman, "did you ask someone with Le Corbusier's non-Catholic background to design and build you a Catholic church? Why didn't you ask a Catholic architect?"

"Had we chosen a Catholic architect," he replied, "we would have had another ugly Sacré Coeur de Montmartre on our hands!"

Coiffes

One of the charming aspects of French provincial society in the years following the second world war, as I discovered on many trips through every corner of France, was the persistent popularity of traditional folk art. That meant dancing, singing, and wearing regional costumes, as the young Frenchwomen from the southwestern region around Perigord demonstrate in this photograph. Further north in Brittany, Breton women still put on voluminous headdresses or coiffes that can't be reconciled with entering an automobile.

Once, during a reportage on brandy in Cognac, I was given a handsome album describing every aspect of the after-dinner beverage from the vine to the table. One photograph left me perplexed. It showed a pretty grape-picker in a harvesting scene. She was wearing a coiffe or headdress made of wooden slats and cotton cloth. If there was too much sun or wind, the slats with cotton covering could be pulled down to protect her face and neck. The coiffe was called a "quichenotte."

What was a quichenotte? Certainly no relation to a quiche lorraine. I stopped for lunch at a restaurant in nearby Jarnac. I showed the waitress the picture but she had no idea what the word meant. The restaurant owner was no better informed, but suggested that I not have coffee in his restaurant but walk down the street.

"There is a lawyer there who is the author of your album," he explained. "When he sees you with his album, he will undoubtedly invite you in for a coffee."

He did.

"What is the origin of the word 'quichenotte?'" I inquired. The lawyer smiled and said the explanation was simple.

"When the English soldiers were retreating through Aquitaine back to England during the 100 Years War," he said, "naturally they tried to embrace the pretty Frenchwomen in the vines. Well, the coiffes got in the way. So, the soldiers called them 'kiss-me-nots.' You know how words get deformed from one language to another. So, kiss-me-nots were turned into French 'quichenottes.'"

Name-Dropping and Dropping Names

The rigidity of the French authorities in regard to the first name of newborn children dates back hundreds of years to the Bourbon monarchy. Through the centuries, the Catholic Church controlled the registry of births and the names of babies. Parents had to choose a Christian name, generally from the calendar of saints.

The French revolutionaries of 1789 ended all that by abolishing the calendar of saints and creating a "revolutionary calendar" based on the seasons, weather and harvesting. The decree of November 24, 1793 left parents pretty much free to name their baby as they wished.

But not for long. On September 9, 1805, Napoleon signed a law abolishing the revolutionary calendar and brought back the Roman Catholic calendar of saints. Henceforth, all children had once again to be named for a saint.

Any attempt to name a child in a whimsical or fanciful manner was firmly and sternly rejected by the town clerk in the city hall. There was no room for fantasy in names, especially names that might handicap or harm or ridicule a child later on in life. These were invariably turned down.

The philosophical justification for the state, rather than the father and mother, judging the reasonableness of a first name derived from the conviction in France that children were citizens and enjoyed the protection of the state. Parents were less trustworthy. If one may paraphrase the axiom that wars were too serious an affair to be entrusted to generals, naming a child was too serious a matter to be entrusted to parents.

Not that all French parents readily accepted this idea. Indeed, ever since Napoleon's decree in 1805 parents have fought with city hall authorities to be able to name their children as they wish. After failing to get anywhere in French courts, irate parents took their case to international tribunals like the European Court of Human Rights, where they were no more successful.

During the de Gaulle years one father tried to name his daughter "Gaullette." The town clerk said, "No, that's not a name, it's a profession of political faith."

Town clerks could be perfect authoritarian bureaucrats as I discovered when, in the 1950s, I tried to give two of my three children bilingual names—Colin and Coralie—and the youngest a well-known, albeit then rarely given, French name, Manon.

"Colin isn't a French name," I was told at the town hall of Boulogne-Billancourt, a Paris suburb. "Neither is Coralie. Furthermore, there was no Saint Colin or Saint Coralie." I replied, "Nonsense. There is a Colin in a novel by Boris Vian and a Coralie in Balzac. It's not my fault if you haven't read them," I snapped. "And anyway I'm not French, I'm American."

Manon was the heroine of a famous novel, "Manon Lescaut," not to mention fine operas by Massenet and Puccini, but neither in the book nor in the calendar of saints was there a Saint Manon. I don't think I would have prevailed with my three names had I been French.

In the snail-pace liberalizing approach some years ago, Judge Robert Sévenier issued instructions to every town hall in France, tens of thousands of them, telling them to consider family history and local usage in judging the acceptability of a proposed name.

That meant, for example, that William, frequently chosen in the region of Bordeaux with its strong historical English influence, was acceptable. It didn't have to be Guillaume. Paraphrasing Sam Goldwyn, nowadays every Tom, Dick and Harry is named Guillaume.

"But why can't you allow parents to choose the names of their own children?" I asked Judge Sévenier. "Isn't France the country of liberty?"

"Because parents can't be trusted," the chief arbiter of name-dropping replied. "They often give absurd names to their children."

Give me an example, I persisted.

"Well, there was a family named Terrieux and they named their two sons Alain and Alex. Get it? Alain Terrieux [à l'intérieur—inside] and Alex Terrieux [à l'extérieur—outside]. Why are you laughing? It's not funny!"

The judge's story reminded me of an hotelier in Savoy named Cocu (cuckold). It's not a rare name in France. He named his son Parfait. Parfait Cocu obviously translates into Perfect Cuckold. When I sent this to Time, I received an immediate query: "Was there a Saint Parfait to be found on the calendar of saints?" I telephoned a Dominican monastery to learn if there had been a Saint Parfait. Indeed, there had been, but he was known in the 4th century when he was stoned to death as Saint Perfectus. Far from being what the French call "un illustre inconnu" (an illustrious unknown), Saint Perfectus has received his share of reverence through the centuries.

Still, it seems to me that calling one's son a perfect cuckold qualifies as an excellent example of a name that would ridicule the man all his life.

Finally, in 1966 the worm turned. On April 12 a ministerial decree declared that first names could be found in mythology, such as Hercules and Achilles and Diane, or be regional names, for example, Breton or Provencal ones, or hyphenated names like Jean-Jacques and Marie-France. Even diminutives were acceptable in certain cases.

Fifteen years later, in 1981, a high court ruled that parents could choose almost any name providing that "in the interest of the child the name was not considered ridiculous." The court also pointed out that there was no official list of acceptable names. In effect, that killed off the calendar of saints as the touchstone.

During these years American television programs, "Dallas," for instance, became popular in France, and French parents liked the idea of giving American names to their children. At the same time a great many North African Muslims emigrated to France and they obviously preferred to name their children Ali and Mohamed rather than Claude and Pierre. All these parents were given carte blanche to name their children as they wished, always providing that they were not silly or ridiculous.

A new article in the Civil Code in 1993 not only virtually authorized the choice of any name by the parents but obliged the town hall clerk, who didn't like the choice, to inform the regional prosecutor. The state's attorney had then to decide whether to initiate legal proceedings to try to get the name tossed out. The burden of trying to refuse a child's first name had, happily and reasonably, shifted in 200 years from the parents to the state.

Roots in France

My decade of reporting from the Riviera coincided with the early growing-up years of my three French-speaking children, Colin, Coralie and Manon. Through them I acquired roots in French society. They helped me to find stories and to cover events I might not otherwise have known about.

Like most children they devoured comic books, and like many parents I deplored this. But one day they pounced on me, waving a "B.D." (bande dessinée, French for comic books) at me. "You have to write about Astérix, he's a national hero," they all shouted.

"Who the devil is Astérix?" I asked. Well, I found out and proposed a story about Astérix to the political section of Time. Why the political section? Because Astérix, like de Gaulle, wanted foreigners out of his country. For de Gaulle, the patriotic Frenchman, it was the Americans. For Astérix, the patriotic Gaul, it was the Romans.

It took eight weeks to persuade editors in New York finally to publish an article on Astérix. It was the first big story to appear in the United States about France's new national hero. I could see myself spending my life on a Greek island basking in the sun and translating an endless stream of Astérix books. Alas, it never happened. Astérix's creators, René Goscinny and Albert Uderzo, found two much more qualified translators in England.

Manon recalled the numerous "Yank, Go Home" signs around her public school in Antibes. "So it was embarrassing when Daddy picked us up after school and insisted on speaking English with us. But we explained to our classmates that our father would not have to go home to America because he was British."

A Stuck Zipper

For the 80th birthday of Nadia Boulanger, a famous musician, composer and teacher, the music world organized a gala event at the Monte Carlo Opera House. When I was assigned to cover it, I learned it was a very formal occasion and I needed a tuxedo. I didn't have one, so I bought one at an elegant store in Paris.

It was a cool December evening on the Riviera and I put on a light overcoat. Arriving in Monaco and parking near the opera house and the Hotel de Paris, I buttoned up. I suddenly noticed that my fly was open. I pulled on the zipper but it didn't budge. I pulled up harder with the same result. I got out of the car to get more leverage, but the zipper didn't move.

What to do? I decided to go to the men's room at the Hotel de Paris where I knew there would be a woman attendant of a certain age. The French poet, Jacques Prévert, called her "Notre Dame du Lavabo" (Our Lady of the Wash Basin).

I entered a stall and said to the woman, "I have a problem. Perhaps you can help me. My zipper refuses to zip."

"Pass your trousers over the door and I'll repair the zipper," came the encouraging reply. But 10 minutes later the attendant was obliged to say, "I'm sorry, but I can't fix it. It's stuck, it's broken."

"Not possible," said I, "it's brand new, I've never worn those pants."

"There's only one thing to be done if you really must go to the Boulanger gala," she said. "You pee as much as you possibly can now and then I'll sew you up in the trousers. But you'll have to stay that way until you get home."

I wasn't comfortable but it worked. The next day I wrote a sizzling letter to the Paris store. They agreed to repair the zipper or replace it. And they did.

I carried that tuxedo with me from one country to another, from one house to another, kept it hanging in a clothes closet but never once put it on. No occasion, no necessity.

One day 35 years after the tuxedo fiasco, in a moment of inexcusable vanity, I decided to see whether I had put on too much weight to fit in those pants. I eased myself into them with no difficulty and, pleased with myself, I pulled up the zipper. Difficult as it is for anyone to believe (myself included), the zipper did not zip, not a centimeter. It was stuck. Well, the tux still hangs in my closet but I've never put it on again.

Mister Huu

(The following story was written—and published—in the 1960s. In those years political correctness, women's lib and date rape were unknown. Although such an article would not be acceptable today, it is an excellent illustration of how changes in society alter journalism and journalists' approach to a story.)

"Would you like a chocolate, Madame?" asked the elegantly-dressed Vietnamese gentleman in impeccable French as the Paris-St. Gervais express pulled out of the Gare de Lyon at 11 p.m. on Friday. What Friday? Any Friday night in 1964, for commuter Truoc Nguyen Huu never missed his train.

Now who can say "No" to a chocolate bonbon, especially when offered with exquisite Asian politeness? Since Mr. Huu's chocolates contained enough dope to lull any woman to sleep 15 or 20 minutes after she had eaten one, the Frenchwoman was soon fast asleep. And that's when the "fun" started. Or at least Huu's fun, certainly not the woman's.

As Frenchwoman Huguette Munck, wife of a gendarme, would later describe her voyage with Huu: "I was sitting alone in a second-class compartment (seating eight) when a Vietnamese gentleman asked if he might sit down. I told him all the seats were free, so he sat down. We talked, as travelers do, about nothing at all.

"Then he began placing things on all the free seats on his side: his raincoat, his briefcase, a newspaper, a book. He explained that he was making an overnight trip and hoped nobody else would enter the compartment so that he might lie down and sleep.

"He inquired where I was going and when I said Annecy, he said, 'What a coincidence, that's where I'm going, too.' He didn't have a ticket though, because when the conductor passed, I recall he said he had lost his ticket and he bought one for Annecy.

"The gentleman first offered me a sugar-coated almond, explaining that he had just come from a friend's wedding. Then he offered me a Suchard chocolate and politely warned me that I might find it a little bitter. I did, but I liked it and ate it. After a while I became sleepy."

Waking up, the gendarme's spouse said: "I noticed at once that he had changed seats and was now sitting directly opposite me. He had removed his suit coat and was wearing a kind of red undershirt. Then I observed that he had taken off his shoes and socks and was barefooted. But I felt too groggy to say or do anything. I soon fell asleep again. When I woke up this time, the man's toes were tickling my legs. Naturally I moved. But I was feeling increasingly groggy. I realized something was happening, but I was unable to react. The next time I awakened from my daze the lights were out (except for a permanently lit, dim ceiling bulb), and the shades were drawn. I found my fellow traveler's toes in my left hand, tickling the palm. I moved my hand at once. Then I seemed to go off to sleep again and when I came to, I discovered that man's toes in my mouth."

At this point, I must tell you who Huu was. As you might expect, he is not to be found in Who's Who or even in Huu's Huu. No, Truoc Nguyen Huu was born in the North Vietnamese city of Dong Tao Dong. He went to France in the middle of World War II (1943) to study medicine. He did so for two years. In 1945 Huu married a well-off, 19-year-old Frenchwoman named Denise de Lodère whose mother owned an antique shop on Boulevard Raspail in Paris's Left Bank. They soon had a daughter who went on to study law.

For some reason Huu abandoned his medical studies, preferring the career of a highly placed employee in a house of commerce. Speaking flawless French and excellent English, Huu became invaluable to the firm's import-export section, particularly in relations with the customs authorities. After 10 years as a "model employee," Huu was found to have pocketed $12,000 intended for the company's cash register. Faced with sacking and scandal, Huu convinced his mother-in-law to co-sign a pledge to pay back the firm. In time, he fully repaid the debt. He left the company two years later in 1956, but thanks to the classified ads of Le Figaro, shortly found employment with a firm in Annecy near the French Alps, doing the same kind of work.

In Annecy, too, Huu was highly regarded by his employers until, that is, he was arrested for stealing a bottle of whisky in a supermarket. Huu paid the court a fine of $100 for the bottle of scotch and, pressed by the firm, resigned his position.

No matter. The Figaro was there with its want ads and in no time at all Mr. Huu had an important position with the John Deere Company at Fleury-les-Aubrais on the outskirts of Orleans. There, too, Huu was considered a model employee. Every Friday afternoon he took the train to Paris where his wife continued to live, dined with her, and then caught the overnight train to the Alps where, he explained, he had work to do. Back in Paris on Sunday to spend the day with his wife, he took a fast train to Orleans on Monday morning to arrive on time at his desk.

When Madame Munck staggered off the train the next morning still dizzy and dazed, Huu was nowhere to be seen. Huguette Munck was, of course, only one of an uncountable number of women who encountered Mr. Huu on the Friday night St. Gervais express, ate his chocolate bonbons, dozed off and were toed.

On one occasion an indignant and apparently insufficiently doped woman made the train conductor escort Huu and her to the police commissariat in the Gare de Lyon. "This vile individual took advantage of me after doping me with a chocolate candy," she exclaimed to the police sergeant. "Doped you with *what*?" asked the cop, shooing her away, as Mr. Huu walked off.

As a rule, Huu operated upon one woman sitting alone in a compartment. But the presence of other passengers, men or women, did not inhibit him. He merely varied his opening gambit. To men he offered a hard mint candy known appropriately as "Bêtises de Cambrai" (follies of Cambrai), while to women he would say: "Mesdames, for you I have something better" and he brought out a box or cellophane bag of gold paper-wrapped Suchard chocolates. Such are—or should we say Suchard—the risks of accepting chocolate candy from a stranger that all who ate them were knocked groggy, while the men remained perfectly lucid. Huu selected his victim and "toed" her as fellow male travelers sought to pierce the darkness to see what Huu was doing. Why didn't anyone protest or attempt to stop Huu? "Apparently because they wanted to see the show," suggested police inspector Marc Pavia, adding that the peeping tom or voyeur instinct is a pretty universal one.

On occasion, though, passengers objected to Huu's behavior. Once Huu fell upon a couple of honeymooners returning from Paris. Did that perturb him? Not a bit. Mint for the husband, chocolate for the wife. Huu concentrated on the woman. Inexplicably, the husband contented himself with muttering, "Hey, you, cut that out!" Unabashed, like the New York City Police Department, Huu kept on toeing away. That was too much for the husband who fetched the train conductor and complained to him about Huu's behavior. "What are you doing to that woman?" demanded the conductor. "Oh, perhaps I have slightly exceeded the bounds of proper conduct," allowed Mr. Huu politely. "Do excuse me. I shall move to another compartment." He did, and no one bothered him any further. "I'll never understand why that silly husband didn't haul Huu off and knock him into slumberland, too," remarked Inspector Pavia who questioned both husband and wife.

Once Huu found himself in a compartment with five women. To each he offered a chocolate. All found the taste terribly bitter and while Huu was in the train corridor, one woman said aloud, "Why, aren't these chocolates simply dreadful! I am going to show mine to a friend who is a pharmacist at home." Her words set a Megève shopkeeper, Madame Grosset Grange, to thinking. She took the half-eaten bonbon out of her mouth, wrapped it in her handkerchief, later put it in a drawer at home, and forgot all about it.

In the spring and summer of the year, half a dozen Frenchwomen lodged formal complaints with police commissariats in Paris and the region of St. Gervais-Annecy. The complaints had several things in common: sleep-giving chocolates, an "Asiatic," and "toes." But Paris and provincial police didn't coordinate their information, there were many Asians in France, and soporific chocolates sounded far-fetched. So Huu toed away. Sometimes he even succeeded in escorting his train companion to a hotel. One such success proved Huu's undoing.

On Friday night, August 28, a 23-year-old divorcee, Yvonne Boullin found herself sharing a second-class compartment with Huu. Chocolates, doping, toes, and Yvonne rode past her stop, Annecy. "Zut!" she cried. "I feel terrible, my head's in a whirl." Huu helped her off the train at Le Fayet. "I'll take you to a hotel where you can sleep it off," said Huu, calling a taxi. Arriving at the Hotel Terminus, Huu asked for a room for the weary traveler whom he started calling by the familiar "tu" and "toi" (thee and thou), suggesting that they were married or lovers. It was eight in the morning. At 11 o'clock Yvonne woke up in bed with Huu lying next to her.

They went downstairs where Huu ordered a taxi to go to the railroad station barely a hundred yards away. His victim ran into the kitchen and whispered to the bewildered hotel owner Fernand Tairraz: "That man has drugged me! I have never seen him before. Call the gendarmerie!" When the taxi arrived, Huu confidently said "A la gare" (To the station), but Madame Boullin murmured in the driver's ear, "I've been drugged by this man. Take us to the gendarmerie at St. Gervais." Which is precisely what the taxi driver did. Huu made no effort to get out of the cab when he saw it head in the opposite direction from that of the station. After all, he had bluffed his way out of one police station, and many a mess on the train.

Most unfortunately for Huu, he had neglected to throw away one chocolate bonbon which police found in a pocket. "If these chocolates are not doped," Inspector Pavia challenged Huu, "then eat this one!" Huu put his hand out to take the chocolate when Pavia suddenly realized the danger. "Mon dieu," he said to himself, "I mustn't let him swallow Exhibit A. It's the only proof we have." And he held on to the chocolate. Analysis by a laboratory in Lyons later revealed that the chocolate contained a dose of a sleep-giving drug inserted by a needle. One of Huu's chocolates, which he never touched himself, was enough to knock out any human being. A search of Huu's pockets also turned up a reduced fare railroad commuter's ticket. With the 50% he saved on fares, Huu later said he could afford to buy chocolate candy at the Gare de Lyon station.

And the Megève shopkeeper who had preserved her half-eaten bonbon read about the "Asian chocolate seducer" in the press, and proudly handed the candy over to the juge d'instruction (investigating magistrate), Ilda Di Marino, in Bonneville, near Annecy. Analysis of that chocolate produced the same results as the confiscated bonbon: it contained a sleep-giving drug. Fast-acting (finally) police under Inspector Pavia tested Yvonne Boullin's urine at a nearby hospital where she was recovering and discovered traces of the same drug.

Seeing stories about Mr. Huu here and there in the papers, women all over France wrote or went to the police to say: "I know that bounder. He drugged and toed me, too." Inspector Pavia called upon 10 of the victims to question them. They included married, single and divorced women, pretty and plain. Many blushed when Pavia went into detail about Huu's behavior. So he showed them Huguette Munck's written statement and asked them to comment on it. Their reply was, "That is just what happened to me."

After a 10-week investigation, Judge Di Marino summoned 10 women plaintiffs. From Brittany, Reims, Lille, Alsace, Paris and the Alps, they traveled to the little courthouse at Bonneville whose only previous claim to judicial glory was the pre-war Stavisky scandal trial. One by one, the Frenchwomen were brought face to face with Mr. Huu. "Do you recognize this man?" Judge Di Marino asked Arlette, an 18-year-old bakery salesgirl. "Oui, c'est bien lui," (Yes, that's him all right) she replied. Then the judge asked Huu if he recognized the young woman. Huu shrugged his shoulders and said, "I am not a physiognomist."

When Arlette recounted this bit of dialogue to her fellow victims in the courthouse, the woman whose honeymooning husband had been so weak-kneed against strong-toed Huu snorted: "Eh bien, he may not be a physiognomist, but my husband certainly is!"

To the ritual question, "Were you on the Paris-St. Gervais express on the night of . . . ?" Huu replied: "Cela se peut" (Could be). Getting hot under his white collar at one point, Huu started to take off his coat. "Keep it on," snapped the judge, "this is a courtroom not a cloakroom."

All day long from 10 a.m. to 9 p.m., with the traditional two-and-a-half-hour break for lunch, the victims pointed accusing fingers at Huu. They experienced no difficulty in recognizing him. Finally, the judge lodged formal charges against Mr. Huu: "offense to decency" and "administering a substance harmful to the health." If convicted, Huu faced a maximum sentence of five years in prison. His lawyer, Joseph Faletti, hoped to get him off much more lightly.

Four months later a black mariah pulled up in front of the gray and white stone courthouse in Bonneville and out stepped the elegantly-dressed, smiling Huu and two unsmiling gendarmes. They came from the jail in Annecy where Huu had spent almost seven months waiting for the trial. As a photographer took pictures, Huu hid his face behind a newspaper.

At 9 a.m. Huu was led into the courtroom. Several dozen spectators stood in the rear. Huu's eyes wandered over the white ceiling, the gold and green wallpaper, the parquet floor and the highly varnished pine benches. There sat

10 lawyers. Their long black cloth robes, white bibs and false ermine (rabbit fur) trimmings lent them the appearance of 17th century Calvinist preachers.

Chief Judge Guy Fourcade disposed of several other cases, then called Huu to the witness stand, which consisted of five iron bars imbedded in the parquet floor and upon which rested a wooden bar. "Until now you have consistently denied giving doped chocolate to women in a train and then committing indecent acts with them in public," began Judge Fourcade. "What is your line today?"

Huu replied softly: "I admit that I administered substances dangerous to the health and committed indecent acts in public. But I didn't steal 300 francs [$60] from a woman as I am accused of doing." Huu used the terms of the formal charges against him. His spoken French was as fine as the cut of his clothes: a delicate pinstripe, dark gray double-breasted suit (rather better tailored than Charles de Gaulle), a black and white tie, a white-on-white shirt with French cuffs, and black shoes. In the only serious questioning of the day, the presiding magistrate brought out Huu's past.

Of the 10 women who formally brought charges against Huu, it turned out that one had emigrated to the Côte d'Ivoire, five were on hand, and four didn't show up.

The judge called Yvonne Boullin to the witness stand to explain why she was demanding damages of $1,000. Then District Attorney René Deleuze stood up and said: "I ask you to pronounce a huis clos." While the courtroom buzzed with the protests of journalists and the sighs of disappointment of spectators, Judge Fourcade immediately agreed with the D.A. and ordered the courtroom cleared. The request for a closed session surprised everyone, except possibly Judge Fourcade since the night before the trial he dined at the Hotel Sapeur in Bonneville with District Attorney Deleuze.

Yvonne Boullin, 5'8" tall, looked down at 5'2" Huu. Soberly she recounted her harrowing night in the train with Mr. Huu and her rude awakening in bed with him the next morning. Did Maître Faletti, Huu's lawyer, cross-examine her? "Oh, no," said Faletti. "It's not at all a good idea to question a prosecution witness. Such questioning almost always backfires." Witness Boullin complained to the judge, "For some time I have been followed around Annecy by two Vietnamese in a car." Nobody asked her further questions about that.

The judge then called upon witness Jacqueline Deleplanque of Mons-en-Baroeul near Boulogne in northern France to describe her "toes-in-the-night" experience with Huu, but the 19-year-old Frenchwoman, who had asked for $800 damages, was not present.

Questioning Huu closely to keep him on his toes, Judge Fourcade asked him to explain who or what gave him the idea of putting young women to sleep and taking advantage of them on trains. Huu, who read Hemingway, Faulkner and Steinbeck in the original English, replied: "The idea came to me from reading about heroes who doped and seduced women in American books." He cited no titles.

Yvonne Boullin's attorney, Raoul Bozon, President of the Lawyers Association of the Haute Savoie Department, exclaimed: "Mr. Huu is a North Vietnamese who has been intoxicated by the Americans, but in his case, only by their literature."

While the judge was reading long excerpts from the statement of Huguette Munck to the investigating magistrate, she was pacing the courthouse corridor impatiently waiting to testify. She wanted to tell the judge of her indignation. Two other of Huu's victims, Monique Schule from nearby Sallanches, and Alice Gales with her husband Gabriel from the Ardennes in eastern France, chatted somberly with Huguette.

Meanwhile at the huis clos trial, Maître Faletti was defending Mr. Huu. "Only two of the 10 complaints are really serious," he declared. "Madame Munck's and Madame Boullin's. As for the other women, it was all very banal. He caressed these women, all right. But after all, that's a nightly occurrence in every neighborhood movie house in the world. Yes, he administered dangerous substances, and the doped bonbons caused vomiting and headaches, but certainly nothing serious. Besides, Mr. Huu has more than paid his debt to society since he has already spent almost seven months in prison, forfeited $3,000 in salary, and lost his job. That's enough. I ask the court to let Mr. Huu go home today a free man."

"It was a very strange case," commented one colleague. "Oh, I am used to curious cases," replied Faletti. "The other day I represented the French Society for the Prevention of Cruelty to Animals against a man named Félix Le Chat [the cat] who mistreated dogs."

One hour and 20 minutes had passed, and the three witnesses were still waiting to be called to the stand when the huissier (court clerk) opened wide the courtroom doors and cried, "Entrez, tout le monde." The trial was over, and the judges were deliberating. "What about me?" Huguette asked angrily. "I didn't get to say anything!" Meanwhile, Mr. Huu was holding court, so to speak, for reporters from his defendant's bench, replying affably in French and English.

Huu pointed to an article about himself in a local newspaper which described the "affaire du petit chocolatier" (the little chocolate-maker's affair) as "rocambolesque" (slapstick). Said Huu: "That's the word for this affair, 'rocambolesque.' You journalists have fertile imaginations." Retorted a reporter: "Maybe, but not as fertile as yours." Huu replied: "You're not reporters, you're novelists." A reporter snapped back, "Well, give us your factual version of this affair." Said Huu: "There are as many versions of this affair, as there are women. Only one woman testified against me. In this trial a mountain gave birth to a mouse."

The judges filed in after only 10 minutes of reflection. Huu stood at the bar awaiting their verdict. "We find you guilty of administering substances dangerous to the health, and of outraging public decency. We acquit you of charges of stealing $60. We sentence you to 10 months in prison [the D.A. had asked for at least a year], and order you to pay Madame Boullin $600 in damages and Mademoiselle Deleplanque $300."

Faletti comforted Huu who had hoped to be sentenced to the exact period he had already spent behind bars. "Huu got off very well," was the verdict of Bonneville lawyers. Faletti added, "10 victims, 10 months in prison, one month for each woman."

As Huu walked off between two gendarmes, Huguette Munck wailed: "What about me? I didn't get a centime." Well, it turned out that the court clerk had *forgotten* to call Huguette, Monique Schule and Alice Gales.

A Proud Spaniard

What have the Spaniards to be so proud of, I asked Emile Cioran, a Romanian philosopher, writer and storyteller. The inquisition, their treatment of the Indians in the Americas and the Jews in Spain, the murder of the great poet, Garcia Lorca, Franco's repressive regime?

"I can't tell you why they feel so proud, or why we refer to them as 'proud Spaniards,'" Cioran admitted, "but I can tell you a story that confirms that they are very proud.

"There was a Spanish noble who lived in a castle on top of a hill. Once a week, always on a Tuesday afternoon, a beggar came to visit him for alms. This went on for years. One day, but it was a Monday morning, the beggar turned up.

"'What are you doing here today on a Monday morning? You know you're supposed to show up only on Tuesday afternoons! What's the matter with you?' demanded the noble angrily, 'have you gone mad?'

"'Oh, if you are going to talk to me in that tone of voice,' replied the beggar just as angrily, 'you'll have to find yourself another beggar!'"

*   *   *

Harmonious Jingling Upon Words

I don't cotton to woolly people

The clone ranger or heigh-ho silvaculture

The only good Indian is a red Indian

The only thing I don't like about cleanliness is that it's next to godliness

What I think about Wagner?—Lohengrin and bear it

Offenbach and often it's not

Long Memories

Between the fourth and fifth crusades to take the Holy Land back from Islam in the early 1200s, Pope Innocent III, whose name belied his activities, ordered a crusade in 1209 against his fellow Christians in Languedoc, now southwestern France.

He was motivated by his fear of the Albigensian "heretics," also known as the Cathars. Highly critical of the church's morality, rather like pre-Protestants 300 years before the Reformation, the Cathars had become increasingly popular in a vast area around Toulouse, Albi (which gave the Albigenses their name), Béziers, Narbonne, Carcassonne and the Pyrenees.

Also deeply worried by the spread of heresy, the (French, not Spanish) Dominican Inquisition had earlier tried to stamp it out. "Do you think that man [never mind a woman] has a soul?" a future Pope of Avignon liked to ask suspected heretics. The answer often led straight to the stake. "Yes, if he has enough to eat in his stomach."

"These heretics are worse than the [Muslim] Saracens," said Pope Innocent III of the Cathars in Languedoc and Provence.

In summoning the people in northern France and nearby countries to extirpate a heresy worse than that of the Infidel, the Pope urged the King of France, Philippe-Auguste, to lead the crusade. He declined and the church assumed direct responsibility when the Abbot of Citeaux, Arnaud Amaury, took command.

Usually, the Pope could make the rulers of France, England, Spain and Germany grovel by threats of excommunication, but he knew he could not force Count Raymond VI of Toulouse and the Languedocian nobility to persecute the heretics.

The reason was that the heresy was too deeply rooted in every class of southern society—the nobility, prosperous burghers, craftsmen, poor urban dwellers, peasants, and both the lower and upper Roman Catholic clergy.

As early as 1202 Cathars were being burned at the stake in Languedoc. The sect recruited members everywhere. Sympathizers were naturally more numerous than actual members of the church, and when a southerner was neither a Cathar nor a sympathizer, he was generally very tolerant of them.

Typical of the southerners' attitude was this reply by Chevalier (Knight) Pons Adhémar to Bishop Foulques of Toulouse who had urged him to persecute the heretics: "We cannot. We were brought up with them. We have relatives among them, and we see them living honestly."

A wealthy old merchant of Toulouse, Pierre Mauran, was exiled for three years in the Holy Land by the church for associating openly with the Cathars. When he returned, he received a hero's welcome, and independent-minded citizens promptly elected him a city councilman.

The south was "rotted by heresy," as Rome saw it.

To make matters worse the Catholic Church was particularly corrupt and weak, and despised in Languedoc. Saint Bernard himself, when preaching in the Midi (southern France) in 1145, expressed pious consternation: "The basilicas are without the faithful, the faithful without priests, and the priests without honor."

By contrast the Cathars had a lofty morality. The Catholic Church implicitly recognized their extraordinary purity when Saint Dominic went about barefoot, preaching and begging for food, to defeat the heresy "with its own arms."

So blatant was the contrast between the pure Cathar clergy and the scandalously corrupt Catholic clergy that southerners used to remark at the sight of a priest, "I would rather be a Jew!"

The Cathars condemned the vengeful God of the Old Testament. They made the New Testament accessible to believers by translating it into Occitan, the Languedocian language. The center of their cult was the "Pater," also translated into Occitan. Instead of "daily bread" Cathars said "suprasubstantial bread."

Even before the crusade and the persecutions, the Cathars had no great cathedrals or parish churches. Ceremonies were generally held in private homes. In large cities, however, they did have their own mission houses where they taught their doctrine, cared for the sick and lived as a community. Prayer rooms had bare, usually whitewashed walls, a few benches and a table covered by an immaculately white cloth. On it lay the Holy Scripture. There were no exterior signs of the cult other than innumerable white candles symbolizing the flames of the Holy Spirit.

In their simplicity, and in their vegetarian and pacifist convictions, the Cathars remind one of the Quakers and some other Protestant sects.

The strength of the faith of the Cathar clergy was nothing short of phenomenal. For although thousands of them were tortured and burned alive, the Inquisition's and the church chroniclers' records of the whole crusade and the decades of persecution that followed mention only one "bonhomme" (a simple preacher) who abjured his faith to save his life. In this respect, too, the Cathars called to mind the early Christian martyrs.

The contrast between northern and southern French societies was great. The free-thinking character of the south and the hidebound nature of the feudal north were well illustrated by their attitudes toward the teaching of philosophy. In Paris the church forbid the study of Aristotle, while at the University of Toulouse the latest Arab discoveries based upon Aristotle were discussed enthusiastically.

Socially, as well as culturally, the south was more advanced than the north. Burghers in the cities of Carcassonne, Toulouse, Béziers, Foix, and many others had won rights and privileges unknown in the north. The position of women was far higher.

As for opulence and wealth, Paris could not compare with Toulouse, nor Rouen in Normandy with Avignon.

The heresy, the riches and the advanced social system were all good reasons for organizing a crusade for Rome and for the northern feudal barons.

A convenient pretext for the crusade was the murder of the papal legate, Pierre de Castelnau, in Saint Gilles by an officer of Raymond VI, Count of Toulouse, on January 14, 1208. In spite of Raymond's public submission to the Church and his flagellation at Saint Gilles in June of that year, an army of crusaders marched on Languedoc to exterminate the heresy and, incidentally, expropriate southern nobles and merchants. The Church promised crusaders indulgences similar to those offered for the much more dangerous and arduous crusade to the Holy Land. No one really knows how large the northern army was—perhaps 20,000 or more—but its size terrified southerners.

On July 22, 1209 the brutal mercenaries of the crusading army broke into Béziers after the city fathers had indignantly refused to save their city and their lives by handing over 222 Cathar heretics.

There followed a fantastic massacre, the memory of which is very much alive today in southern France. Virtually every citizen of the city—around 20,000—was killed, most of them in Catholic churches. Priests with crucifixes, mothers, babies, adolescents, men and women were put to the sword.

Before the massacre a baron is supposed to have asked the Abbot of Citeaux, the crusade's leader and head of one of Christendom's leading monastic orders, the Cistercians, how to distinguish between good Catholics and bad Cathars.

No one knows whether the abbot actually pronounced the famous words attributed to him: "Kill them all, God will recognize his own!"

But that they reflected the abbot's feelings is made perfectly clear from his triumphant letter to the Pope in which he declared that "without regard to sex and age, almost 20,000 of these people were put to the sword."

As chronicles of the time show, even in the brutal Middle Ages the massacre in Béziers revolted the conscience of Europe. One consequence of the deed was to force southern Catholics to ally themselves with the heretics. The crusaders reacted by assuming every southerner was a heretic.

The crusade became a war without mercy. Stakes were lit all over Languedoc, and the region abounded in wretched souls whose eyes had been gouged out, their noses and tongues cut. In a few months southerners hated the northern invaders and their Catholic clergy as intensely as did the peoples of occupied Europe their Nazi oppressors during World War II.

Soldiers of both sides went into battle crying, "Jesus Christ with us!"

Led by Simon de Montfort (whose son, also named Simon, led the baronial opposition to royal encroachment on the privileges gained through the Magna Carta in England in 1264), the crusaders laid siege to and captured cities, citadels and chateaux. Everywhere heretics were burned as monks intoned Latin hymns. Garrisons were coldbloodedly massacred, towns totally demolished. Toward the end of the crusade around 1240, the crusaders adopted a scorched-earth policy and deliberately ruined the entire economy of the south.

Estimates of the total casualties of the crusade either approach or exceed a million, an enormous number for the period.

Little wonder that the name of Simon de Montfort is as unpopular in southwestern France today as that of General Sherman in Atlanta.

I found that out on a visit to Toulouse. Friends arranged a dinner party for me in the Capitole, the center of the city. I found myself sitting next to a Doctor Quercy. "Why did you come to Toulouse?" he asked. "To learn about the Albigensian crusade and to write about it," I replied.

The next day I told my friends how much I liked Dr. Quercy. "Well, he didn't like you at all," came the reply. "What could I have possibly said or done?" I asked. "Dr. Quercy took you for a friend of Simon de Montfort!"

Southern Americans still remember Sherman in Atlanta with anger some 140 years later, but the angry memories of the southern French stretch back almost 800 years!

Romania's Unknown Soldier

A story I wrote about a new book by Romanian writer Emile Cioran had appeared in Time Magazine, so I thought I might ask him to arrange a luncheon with one of his closest friends, the playwright Eugène Ionesco, also a philosopher of the absurd.

The encounter took place at the two Romanians' favorite restaurant, La Coupole at Montparnasse.

In the course of the conversation Cioran said to Ionesco, "Eugène, why don't you tell our journalist friend the story of the Romanian Unknown Solider?" The author of that delicious line, "take a circle, caress it, it becomes vicious," needed no nudging.

"Rather late in the first world war the Romanian General Staff realized that every country involved in the conflict, on both sides, had its Unknown Soldier. But Romania had none. It was decided that our country also deserved one," Ionesco began.

"An elaborate 'celebration,' if you can call it that, was arranged. Ten freshly killed infantry soldiers lay in coffins side by side. The press was there to publicize the event. A troop of Romanian boy scouts was also present. The young scout leader was asked to choose one of the 10 unfortunate men to be Romania's Unknown Soldier. He looked carefully at each man and finally pointed to one of them. The journalists gathered around the scout and asked him what had made him select that particular soldier. He replied, 'Because it was my father.'"

And Ionesco added: "Several months later we read in a Bucharest newspaper a story headlined 'Son of Unknown Soldier Dies in Danube Canoeing Accident.'"

*   *   *

Harmonious Jingling Upon Words

And last, says George Sand, but not Liszt

I don't like fish and chips even when wrapped in The Guardian

Chimay beer has become so popular throughout the world that the Trappist monks who brew it are speechless with astonishment

Noisy Noise Annoys a Bluebird

After builder Einar Rossow had put up an apartment house at the seaside Promenade des Anglais, a choice location in Nice, he discovered he couldn't rent a flat in it. That was because while he was building the Oiseau Bleu (Bluebird), just across the street, so to speak, Nice airport was extending its runways to accommodate bigger jets. Dozens of aircraft landed and took off every day. The noise level was deafening, a 115-decibel din that was 45 decibels above the scientifically established level of human tolerance.

So Rossow sued Air France for damages of around $400,000. "Not us," replied Air France. "We just go where we're told to land and take off. Nice airport is owned by the Chamber of Commerce."

Redirecting his lawsuit, Rossow insisted that the Chamber of Commerce should have informed him of the approaching noise level less than a football field's distance from the windows of his apartments. "How do you expect me to rent my flats in these conditions?" he demanded. "Why didn't you warn me?"

The Chamber of Commerce retorted: "Don't you read Nice Matin? Everyone here reads the local daily newspaper. It has been full of stories about the extended runways. Besides, you could see what was happening with your own eyes."

"I'm not a newspaper reader, I'm a building constructor," maintained Rossow.

The defense cited a 1952 international air traffic treaty that declares "there is no right to damages if the injury results only from the passage of the aerial vehicle through air space in conformity to the applicable traffic rules."

France has never ratified that treaty. So, plaintiff Rossow pointed to a 1924 French law which says that "the right of an aerial vehicle to fly over private property cannot be exercised in such conditions as to interfere with the rights of the proprietor."

An appellate court ruled in Rossow's favor but added that his failure to soundproof the Bluebird apartment house would reduce the still-to-be-determined damages.

Shortly afterwards, Rossow rented most of the apartments in his building . . . to deaf people.

Urbi et Gorby

During his visit to the Pope in Rome Mikhail Gorbachev and John Paul II hit it off very well. On following Sundays, the Pope could easily have altered his Urbi et Orbi blessing from St. Peter's to the faithful in the city and the world to address it to "Urbi et Gorby."

In what language did they converse? Russian, Polish, Latin? John Paul II was a distinguished linguist, while Gorbachev knew only Russian. I organized half a dozen press conferences for him in Brussels, Bern, Amsterdam and Geneva and not once did I ever hear him utter a word of English or French. As a result, these press briefings were painfully slow since so much interpretation back and forth was necessary.

Actually I did hear Gorbachev pronounce two words of English when I handed him some newspaper clippings—"thank you."

Flackery Will Get You Nowhere

As I had worked many years as a journalist and, later, as many more years as a press officer for a score of United Nations and non-governmental organizations, I was asked by an NGO to give a talk about what it was like on both sides of the barricades. What was the best way for UN and NGO press attachés to approach journalists?

I began by saying that a span of 28 years as a print press journalist and foreign correspondent in France does not prepare you for the work of a public information officer in the United Nations in Geneva or anywhere else.

That isn't totally true because in all those years at least you have learned to write a story. That may not seem like much to an ex-journalist, but in the ranks of UN information officers, you encounter surprisingly few who can put to paper a simple feature or press release, much less write their way out of a paper bag.

I found the metamorphosis from a Time Magazine reporter to a United Nations Environment Programme (UNEP) press attaché a painful or, rather, an uncomfortable affair. While distributing UNEP press releases or feature stories to Swiss journalists and foreign correspondents, I found myself saying apologetically, "only last week I was a reporter like you," or, "just last month I was a journalist, too."

That went on for about a year until I reconciled myself to the fact that, whatever anyone else called me, I was no longer a journalist. Like so many newspapermen or women, I had thought there was no life after journalism.

Life after journalism might also have led to advertising or public relations. Without even being a wordsmith one could perhaps sell soap or peddle perfume. The idea of becoming a flack for an oil polluting company, for example, was as abhorrent to me as public relations is to most journalists.

I remember an airline public relations flack wandering around the rue de Berri editorial room of the Paris edition of the New York Herald Tribune one Sunday afternoon. Addressing himself to me as I was the travel editor, he said that one of his airline's trans-Atlantic planes had crashed and he would appreciate it if the headline writer (of the front page story) would mention his airline by its nationality but avoid using its three familiar initials. I shooed him at the news editor who chased him out of the building.

But would the United Nations be a more acceptable employer than a public relations firm? The answer is yes, whatever the very considerable shortcomings and limitations of UN information work are.

It is easier, more honest and more satisfying, I believe, to be "selling," that is to say, publicizing, the environment, health, children, climate change, refugee problems, conditions in the work place, the status of women, the abolition of illiteracy, family planning, all of which are activities and causes of the UN, than promoting consumer products.

For every editor who changes your copy, there must be two or three UN officials who change, denature, destroy your press release or feature. The difference is that editors are professional journalists, while very few UN officials who "clear" copy know anything about journalism or the needs of journalists, or, for that matter, about writing styles.

When I turned up at UNEP, I was very lucky. The European Regional Director, Peter Thacher, was a committed and knowledgeable environmentalist at ease in front of a journalist. When I asked him whether I could or should do this or that, he would reply: "You tell me. We hired you because you were a journalist. You do what you think is good and right and I'll back you up." He did.

Once in Malta at a Mediterranean pollution conference, in a wrap-up press release I listed the participating countries of the basin geographically rather than by the traditional UN practice of alphabetical order. A bureaucrat and self-appointed censor pointed out to me my "mistake." Who looks at a map alphabetically, I asked? What upset the would-be censor was that countries near each other geographically were often hostile to each other. Their feelings could be hurt, he said, and their governments might protest. Protest what, I asked, the absence of alphabetical order?

Press releases are intended for journalists. Peter Thacher knew it, and supported me. For the next seven years I never met a government official or UN official who objected to my preference for geographical listing.

Some time later, on the occasion of a UNEP Caribbean pollution meeting in Managua, Nicaragua, during the contra-Sandinista conflict and US-Cuban tension, I started a press release with these words: "In spite of the conflicts that abound in the Caribbean, most of the countries of the region will meet in Managua, Nicaragua, to see what they can do about the problems of their common sea." Pretty mild and obvious? Not for one UN information officer who scolded me, saying: "You know very well that we don't write about conflicts in press releases." As I knew no such thing, I put out a cleared version of the press release with the "unacceptable" phrase. No one protested.

Another shibboleth of UN information activities is the policy of never mentioning the nationality of an international civil servant in a UN story. On one occasion a very bright official crossed out the name of his country. I objected in vain. When I gave the story to the Geneva bureau chief of the Associated Press, Sandy Higgins, I mentioned the incident and the name of the country. "We have to include the quoted source's nationality in an AP dispatch," he remarked. I recounted this to the UN official and he agreed to a reference to his country.

When I first started writing for UNEP, there was quite a bit of hostility to the use of officials' names. "Just say that the United Nations Environment Programme announced it," I was urged. Sorry, I said, that isn't good enough for most journalists.

Naturally, there was little or no opposition to quoting the organization's top official. Quite the contrary. He (or in rare cases, she) frequently was quoted in the opening paragraph of the UN story, all too often saying nothing newsworthy.

In my first conversation with UNEP's Executive Director, Dr. Mostafa K. Tolba, I pointed out that I had quoted him in a story about the Mediterranean, "Rocking the Cradle of Civilization", toward the bottom of the second page. "I think the quote will get picked up because it says something," I explained, "but it's not strong enough to be in the lead." Dr. Tolba's comment resembled Peter Thacher's: "You're a journalist. I'm a micro-biologist. You do it your way." I believe that established a relationship of mutual confidence.

On another occasion, years later in Montreal at the ozone layer conference, I wrote a press release that contained quite a few factual errors. After Dr. Tolba had read it, he remarked, "There are a lot of mistakes. You journalists often make mistakes; we scientists are supposed to catch them."

Not all bosses are so reasonable. Much depends on how big their endangered ego-system is.

I said earlier that press releases are written for journalists. That sounds obvious but it isn't always the case. On one occasion when I was running the information side of a "prepcom" for Maurice Strong for the Rio Earth Summit, I was asked to put a table in the conference hall for daily press releases. "But the conference delegates will swipe them and there'll be none left for journalists," I objected. An information officer explained, "The press releases are intended for the participants, not for journalists." Q.E.D.

There is certainly no tradition in UN story titles for punning, witticism or humor. The tendency is to write mundane not to say deadly dull headings. But a witty title can put a story across. One example: an article on elephants as an endangered species went out under the title, "Saving Elephants Is a Mammoth Tusk." The Geneva-based BBC correspondent, Martin Sixsmith, liked it, did a story for the "Today" program, and used the joke.

I can't guarantee that stories entitled, "The Chemical Industry and the Environment, or This Little Pigment Went to Market" or, on Siberian tigers,

"Tundra Is the Night, Taiga, Taiga Burning Bright" or even on the Chinese campaign against snails, that is, schistosomiasis or bilharzia, "Red Snails in the Sunset," induced any journalist to do an article on the subject. At least, the titles didn't put journalists to sleep.

Assuming you have a newsworthy story with an enticing title and good, quotes from available experts, how do you go about offering it to journalists?

The UN way is to place it on the racks in two press rooms of the Palais des Nations in Geneva. My way is to hand it out to correspondents, individually, going from door to door, like an encyclopedia salesman. The advantage of my system is that I can discuss the story with journalists, and add information not in the press release, such as the hours of coffee breaks or at what hotel an expert is staying.

There is another advantage. A press release alone is not the best formula for inciting journalists to write stories. But linked to a press conference, the story stands a much better chance of taking off. In making the rounds of correspondents' offices, I get a clear idea of whether they really want a briefing. If they don't, there's no point in scheduling one.

Still another virtue of my door-to-door approach is that I get better acquainted with correspondents than UN information officers are able to do at impersonal briefings for the entire UN system.

The heart of the matter is this: how do you satisfy your United Nations directors and colleagues while you are useful and effective with journalists? And are you doing it in good conscience, your political and moral integrity intact?

Eschewing UN jargon and writing like a journalist is, I think, necessary or at least useful and productive. If a journalist reads your story and, consciously or unconsciously, says to himself, "I could have written that" or simply, "that doesn't read like the conventional UN hand-out," that's a good start. As the saying goes, it takes one to know one.

But how do you get that "journalistic" story past bosses and colleagues? Unfortunately there is no simple answer. Sometimes you can by reasoning with them: this is what journalists really want to read and before you insist on a traditional, wooden press release, let's see whether my "unconventional" one gets widely picked up by the wire services and newspaper correspondents.

If that doesn't work, try to make sure that your story is read and cleared by preferably one or, at most, two clearance-givers. One of my releases was read and approved, virtually untouched, by five censors only to fall victim to a sixth reader. In a rewritten version, a second attempt to win clearance got by three officials, but failed to satisfy a fourth. Meanwhile, of course, the plan to give the press release to journalists two or three days before the opening of the meeting to whet their appetite and to persuade some of them to file week-enders or advance stories had collapsed.

The English proverb, "too many cooks spoil the broth," could hardly be more appropriate. The trouble with the adage in the UN is that no official conceives of himself as the one too many cook.

If you argue that bureaucratic clearance procedures may cost the organization a great deal of favorable publicity, usually you don't get very far. For one thing, many UN officials—and unfortunately that includes quite a few information officers—sincerely believe that "the less that gets into the press the better." How many times have I heard a UN official say, "stay out of the press and stay out of trouble."

That widespread philosophy does discourage me. Fortunately, however, the majority of UN officials and press attachés, with whom I have worked in half a dozen UN agencies and organizations on every continent, believe in speaking frankly to journalists. Yes, journalists sometimes make mistakes in their articles and broadcasts, but it's rarely intentional or malicious and, anyway, do UN officials and scientists never err?

Another characteristic of UN information services is verbal diarrhea. There is a glut of press releases which quote the boss in a meaningless story, e.g., the planting of a tree at organization headquarters by a newly-arrived ambassador. The writer makes sure that his boss sees the press release in which he is quoted, but as no newspaper is likely to publish a story about it, that's the end of the line for that bit of press flackery, or rather fakery. If you enjoy good relations with journalists in your own city and around the world, they will give you published articles or dispatches for their news agency. Even a modest packet of these clippings will impress colleagues and bosses. Distribute one several times and their confidence in you, and your "journalistic" approach, will rise sharply.

In UN "capitals" like Geneva and New York there are usually twice-a-week or daily briefings. Spokespersons for UN organizations vie with each other to promote their activities. In my view, if you haven't got a solid story to push, it's wise to stay away from these encounters with journalists. One day, two journalists came up to me in the Palais des Nations and, saying they hadn't seen me for several weeks, inquired whether I had stopped working. "No," I replied, "I haven't had a good story to sell."

Staff information officers might argue that that policy was easier for a consultant to pursue, but even when I was UNEP's staff information officer in Europe, I followed that line of thinking. I didn't engage in silent acts of presence on podiums. But when I did have a newsworthy story, I wasted no time walking the corridors and popping in on 30 or 40 journalists, one by one.

You ought not to play favorites among journalists. But experience has demonstrated to me time after time that if you hope for worldwide coverage of your meeting or press conference or press release, you won't get it unless either Reuters or the Associated Press, or both, file a story, which is then sent out to newspapers and magazines, television and radio networks throughout the world. The BBC's World Service and Agence France-Presse do have huge international audiences, but for major global coverage there is no substitute for AP and Reuters. You can deplore this state of affairs, but it is a fact of journalistic life. So, I think a slightly more energetic effort to interest these two wire services is justified.

I'd like to come back to the matter of friendship or warm professional relations with journalists. Occasionally, a journalist bumps into me at the post office or press bar in the Palais des Nations and asks, "have you got a story for me today?" or "anything coming up next week?" When you enter a reporter's office, it's agreeable to feel welcome. I take the time to chat about all sorts of subjects with correspondents if they have the time. They size you up and know whether you're serious. Staff press attachés very rarely have, or take, the time to call on individual journalists. The important point is for these journalists to know you have a newsworthy story or you'd not be bothering them. Obviously, your idea and their idea of what constitutes a newsworthy story doesn't always coincide. Generally, though, it does. A cynical UNEP colleague, long since gone from the UN, once told me, "we're old-timers and you and I know we're selling hot air." I've never thought you could peddle hot air to journalists. After all, they are familiar with the product.

A sine qua non of every UN organization's media department is an up-to-date list of journalists. That's easier said than done. The best of media lists is out of date from one day to another. Journalists change jobs, lose jobs, retire and die, and newspapers do, too. Every six months, ideally, but at least every year, lists of journalists need to be checked and revised. Clearly that is a time-consuming and costly affair. Over the years I've done it for UNEP, UNICEF and the World Health Organization. My current media list contains around 800 journalists, specialists in the environment, public health, science, development, or generalists interested in developing countries and international affairs. I reckon I know well perhaps 300 or 400 of them, and have a passing acquaintance with many of the others.

One lacuna in the list was journalists from six former socialist countries of central and eastern Europe. Few UN or non-governmental organizations knew who was who on what publication, TV network or radio station. UNEP sent me to Russia, Poland, Hungary, Romania, Bulgaria and the Czech Republic to identify and meet journalists interested in the environment, science, development and the United Nations. I met and talked individually with 79 of them. Their "isolation," as they put it, ended, and 17 of them participated in a UNEP environmental seminar in Geneva. Naturally, their names are among the 800 and they are receiving press releases, feature stories, documentation, radio cassettes, TV films, etc., from UNEP.

If one may paraphrase the old question—does a waterfall make any noise if there's no one there to hear it?—is there any point in writing UN stories, if there's no one there to receive and use them? Putting out a story on your organization's letterhead paper with liberal quotations by the boss doesn't mean anyone anywhere has used it.

Well, then, is it possible to reconcile the bureaucratic requirements of the UN system with the needs of journalists without selling your soul? I think the answer is "yes," but a lot depends on the common sense of your colleagues and bosses, and on your own courage and competence. Pusillanimity, like flackery, will get you nowhere.

And Every Minute of It Was Hard Work

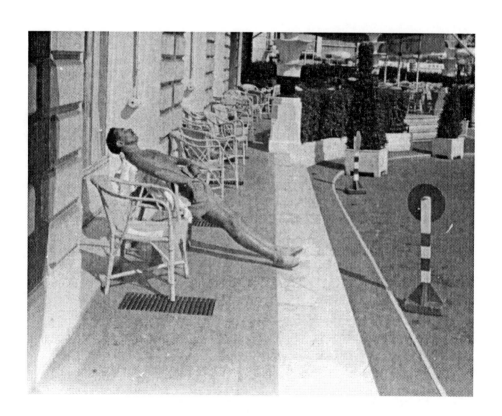

Printed in the United States
66561LVS00002B/1

9 781425 727475